TOWER HAMLETS

91 000 001 161 58 7

KU-863-050

TOWER HAMLETS
LIBRARIES

9100001161587

Bertrams   23/02/2012

J333.791   £8.99

THCUB   TH11001852

Using Energy

Sally Hewitt

W
FRANKLIN WATTS
LONDON • SYDNEY

This edition 2012

Franklin Watts
338 Euston Road
London NW1 3BH

Franklin Watts Australia
Level 17/207 Kent Street
Sydney NSW 2000

Copyright © Franklin Watts 2008

Editor: Jeremy Smith
Art director: Jonathan Hair
Design: Jason Anscomb

All rights reserved.

A CIP catalogue record for this book is available from the British Library.

We would like to thank Jules Dervaes of the Path to Freedom project for
use of his photographs and text relating to solar energy at home.

Picture credits: Alamy: 8b, 10, 11, 15, 16-17, 18-19, 22-23, 24-25,
26-27. Druk White Lotus School: 14. Path to Freedom project: 12-13.
Ramesh Nibhoria: 21. Shutterstock: 3, 7 all, 8t, 9, 11t, 20.

Every attempt has been made to clear copyright. Should there be any
inadvertent omission, please apply to the publisher for rectification.

Dewey Classification: 941.085
ISBN: 978 1 4451 0885 8

Printed in China

Franklin Watts is a division of Hachette Children's
Books, an Hachette UK company.
www.hachette.co.uk

Contents

Energy types

Energy is the power to make things work. Food gives us the energy we need to live, grow and work. Petrol gives a car energy to move and electricity gives a light bulb energy to glow.

Growing demands

As the number of people living on planet Earth grows year after year, the demand for energy grows too. There are more and more people using energy for keeping warm or cooling down, for cooking, for turning on lights and machines and for travelling about. The problem to be solved for the future is how to provide enough energy for a growing number of people while looking after the planet as well.

Challenge!

Write down everything you do that uses these kinds of energy:

- Gas
- Electricity
- Coal
- Wood
- Oil
- Petrol

Think about how much electricity you and your family use every day.

Major cities such as Hong Kong use up huge amounts of electricity every day.

Fossil fuels

Fuel is what we burn to make energy. Oil, natural gas and coal are fossil fuels. They formed from the remains of plants and animals that died millions of years ago. We burn fossil fuels in power stations to make electricity. Petrol is made from oil so we burn fossil fuel when we ride in the car. All this causes the air to become polluted. There is also only a limited amount of fossil fuels left.

Greenhouse gas

As we burn fossil fuels to release energy, smoke from chimneys and exhaust fumes containing a gas called carbon dioxide (CO_2) goes into the air. Carbon dioxide is a "greenhouse gas". It helps to trap heat from the Sun into the Earth's atmosphere and is partly responsible for "global warming", which means making the Earth warmer.

Saving energy

To be a member of the Green Team you need to think about saving energy. Saving energy helps to save fossil fuels and may help reduce global warming.

Action!

Choose one thing you can do to save energy.

• Walk to school.
• Don't leave the television on standby – turn it off.
• Turn lights off in an empty room.
• Get into the habit of doing it every day.
• Now add another action that will save energy.

Global warming is melting ice at the North and South Poles, which causes sea levels to rise. Turtles are threatened by rising seas destroying their nesting beaches.

Coal is burned at this power station to make electricity. Smoke mixed with greenhouses gases such as carbon dioxide pours into the air, causing pollution and contributing to global warming.

Renewable energy

Energy from natural sources, such as wind, sunlight and water, is renewable which means it will never run out. It is clean energy too, because fossil fuels do not have to be burned to produce it.

Wind turbines need to be placed where there is plenty of wind. These wind turbines turn in strong sea breezes.

Wind

Wind turns the blades at the top of wind turbines to generate electricity. One turbine on a wind farm can provide clean electricity for 1,000 households per year. It would need a lot of wind turbines to provide energy for a big city of two million people.

This solar power plant in Germany is one of the biggest in the world. Its panels turn to follow the Sun throughout the day.

Water

Energy from running water, tides and waves can be turned into electricity.

Sun

Solar cells in solar panels turn sunlight into energy. Solar panels are used in power plants to provide electricity for a large number of homes.

Challenge!

Look at all the kinds of natural and renewable energy there are on these pages.

• Find out if any of these kinds of energy are available where you live.

Bio energy

Bio energy is energy stored in plants and animal waste. It is renewable because new plants will grow and animals will make more waste. Biofuel can be burned in power stations. But as it is burned, carbon dioxide escapes into the air. However, biofuel plants take in carbon dioxide as they grow, which helps to reduce the amount of this greenhouse gas in the air.

Geothermal energy

"Geo" means Earth, and "thermal" means heat, so geothermal energy is energy taken from Earth's natural heat. Beneath the surface of the Earth is very hot, liquid rock called magma. Heat from magma can be used to make electricity and to heat water and buildings.

 ## Action!

Choose any of the kinds of energy on these pages and pages 6-7.

• Write a list of points about it that are good for the planet.

• Write a list of points about it that are bad for the planet.

• Would this type of energy provide enough electricity for everyone who needs it?

• Do any kinds of energy have only good points or do any have only bad points?

• Find out about nuclear energy, too. What are the good and bad things about this form of power?

Iceland uses natural geothermal energy to generate electricity and heat its homes and buildings. Steam produced by geysers like this one is turned into clean electricity.

Green energy at home

Have you ever thought about where the electricity and gas that powers and heats your home comes from? Is it from power plants that burn fossil fuel, a nuclear power station or from renewable energy? You can find out, and choose an energy supply that helps to save the planet.

Green supplier

A green electricity supplier will provide electricity from renewable resources – solar, wind, water or bio energy. Green energy is often a bit more expensive, but the extra money supports renewable energy and goes towards research and education. The higher prices should help users try harder to save energy at home!

Challenge!

Find out about your energy supplier.

- Is your heating powered by gas or electricity?
- Can you change to a green supplier if you don't already use one?

Every time you turn on a switch, you use energy.

High winds blow over this home in California, USA, in winter. The extra electricity generated goes towards saving money on electricity bills.

Wind turbine

A turbine on the roof of a house needs lots of wind to make enough electricity. In the right place, it can provide electricity for the home and some to spare. If you live in a windy place, it might be worth having a wind turbine installed on your roof.

Hydro power

Homes near a river or stream may be able to use hydro power. Small water generators, or micro-hydro turbines, can produce enough non-stop energy from running water to power a home.

This river runs all year round creating energy whatever the weather.

Working together

Wind turbines, solar panels and hydro power systems can be expensive to set up. Groups of people living near each other can join together and apply for a grant or invest in a clean, renewable energy source.

Action!

Make a simple solar oven and use solar energy:

You will need:

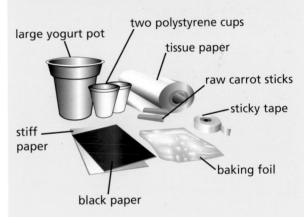

large yogurt pot
two polystyrene cups
tissue paper
raw carrot sticks
sticky tape
stiff paper
baking foil
black paper

1. Line one cup with black paper. Put in the carrot.
2. Cover the sheet of stiff paper with foil, and wrap round the cup to make a cone.
3. Sit the cup in the cone, put this in the other cup and put in the yogurt pot.
4. Stuff tissue paper in the gap between the pot and cup to trap heat in.
5. Place the pot outside and angle the cone towards the Sun. Keep turning to face the Sun to cook the carrot.

The foil directs heat from the Sun into the pot. The black paper soaks up the heat, the tissue paper stops heat escaping and the carrot cooks in half an hour.

Solar energy at home

Jules Dervaes and his family live in an ordinary house in an average city in southern California, USA. They were worried about the future of the planet because they realised that pollution was harming the Earth by causing global warming. So, they asked, "What can we do?"

The solar panels were 826 mm wide by 1575 mm long and weighed 17 kg.

Solar panels

The family decided to install 12 solar panels, specially designed to capture light and turn it into clean, renewable energy from the Sun, instead of using electricity made from dirty fossil fuels.

Professional help

The first problem was that, although the family wanted to do as much of the work as they could by themselves, they still needed expert help and advice. So, they hired a professional electrician to draw up the plans and to help install the panels.

Challenge!

The Dervaes family live in a sunny place, so solar panels make sense.

Find out what kind of renewable energy would be best for the part of the world where you live.

Fitting the panels was slow work at first, until everyone got used to working on the steep, slanted roof.

Fitting the panels

One by one, up went the solar panels. After each panel was bolted in place, the electrical wires were connected to the previous panel. Finally, all the circuits were complete and connected to the main junction box. It was checked by a city inspector and the power was switched on.

The Dervaes family learned that they can do something to help the planet by choosing a clean source of electricity.

After each panel was bolted in place, the electrical wires were connected to the previous panel. Finally, all the circuits were complete and connected to the main junction box.

Mr Dervaes says:

"We strongly believe that we can change our 'footprint' on this Earth. People can make a difference to bring about a bright and sunny future."

The family was thrilled with the final result.

 Action!

The Dervaes family worked together to change how they use energy.

• Have a family meeting and decide how you can work together to change how you use energy and make a difference.

Your school building

When a new school is built, there is a chance to design it as a "sustainable school". Choosing a renewable energy supply is one of the most important ways a new school can care for the environment.

Case study – Druk White Lotus School in the Himalayas

The Druk White Lotus School is high up in a desert environment where temperatures can drop to as low as minus 13° C. It has been built with locally produced, recyclable materials using both traditional building methods and modern, green design and technology.

Heat and energy

The walls are made of granite with a mud centre, a traditional material that insulates the building and helps to keep it warm. Electricity is produced by solar power using solar panels.

Sustainable design

Snow cuts off the school in winter, so it is designed to be self-sustainable all year round.
• The school grows its own food in indoor gardens.
• Fresh groundwater is used and recycled.
• Human waste is treated naturally and recycled.

Local building materials such as stone and wood help the school to blend in with the natural environment.

No electricity

In many communities around the world, there is either no electricity or very little. This may be good for the planet, but not for school children. It means they do not have bright lighting for reading and writing and energy to turn on computers, the Internet or televisions.

Case study – Solar Electric Light Fund (SELF)

SELF is a charity set up in 1990 to help bring solar power to rural areas in developing countries. It is running a campaign to bring electricity into schools, called "Brightening lives with solar schools". SELF's Solar Schools project in South Africa provides schools with solar energy. This is used to power lights, TVs and videos, computer labs of 25-30 workstations, Internet access, and links to high-quality distance learning resources. The solar electricity has helped to improve the lives of 2,000 students.

 # Action!

Raise money for an organisation such as SELF.

These types of organisations install solar or other renewable clean energy in schools in developing countries, giving pupils the opportunity for a modern education in a sustainable way.

Melusi Zwane, Principal at Myeka High School, one of the schools helped by SELF, says:

"The solar power equipment has had a huge impact on the culture of learning and teaching in our school ... The school dropout rate has lowered considerably. You will never understand how much difference the intervention of SELF has made to the education of an African child."

This South African high school is powered by solar electricity.

Save energy at home and at school

Making sure electricity isn't wasted at home and at school is something that all members of the Green Team can do. By getting into new habits, you can set an example to your parents and teachers.

Sara

Turn off lights when you don't need them but don't leave anyone in the dark!

Turn it off!

The little green, red or white lights on your television, DVD player or radio tell you that the machine has been left on standby and is using energy and giving out heat. Agree with your parents and teachers what needs to be left on and what can be switched off when it is not in use.

Phone chargers

Leaving a phone charger plugged in and switched on when it is not in use uses electricity and gives out heat. So switch it off and unplug it when your phone is fully charged.

At school

Schools usually spend more money on their electricity bills than they do on books. Cutting back on the amount of electricity used at school not only saves money that can be spent on books instead, but it also helps to look after the planet at the same time.

Challenge!

Spend at least an hour of your free time without turning on a machine.

• Read, play a board or card game, make something or learn a magic trick instead.

A junior school pupil from Teddington, UK, examines the electronic utilities monitor panel at her school.

A motion sensor turns the lights on when someone is moving in this room, and turns them off when there is no movement.

Case study – An electronic utilities monitor at school

An electronic utilities monitor records power being used and CO_2 emissions throughout the day. The Green Team can make a school energy saving plan, put it into action then use the monitor to check how much energy the school is managing to save and if it is cutting its CO_2 emissions.

Case study – Oregon

Vale Elementary, Middle and High Schools in Oregon, USA, expect to save nearly three-quarters of their electricity bill by putting in energy-saving light bulbs controlled by motion sensors. This was paid for and organised by Oregon Department of Energy.

Vale School Superintendent. Matt Hawley, says:

"We are more than happy with the results. The new lighting is great. Thanks to the motion sensors, lights get turned off now. Before the project, lights would be turned on for a Saturday morning and they'd stay on all weekend."

Action!

Hold an energy week at school. Make a plan of energy saving actions, for example:

- Turn off lights when you leave a room.
- Fit energy-saving light bulbs.
- Shut doors and windows to keep in heat.
- Hold an assembly, invite parents and tell everyone the plans. Check the school's energy for a week. Compare it with energy use during energy week.

Keeping warm

When it is too cold we try to warm up, and when it is too hot we try to cool down. Central heating keeps us warm and air conditioning cools us down. They both use energy. Members of the Green Team look for ways of keeping the correct temperature while also saving energy.

Turn it down! Turn it up!

If you live where it is very cold in winter, you may need to keep the heating on 24 hours a day. If you live where it is very hot, you may have air conditioning to keep you cool. You can save energy by turning the heating down to as low as it is comfortable in the day and even lower at night, and by reducing the air conditioning as much as it is comfortable.

For every degree you turn the heating down or the air conditioning up, you will save money on energy bills!

A thermostat keeps the temperature at the setting you choose. Talk about the thermostat setting with an adult. Don't turn it down yourself.

Challenge!

Warm up or cool down without electricity.

- Wear warm clothes in cold weather and have hot drinks.
- Inside, wear a vest, woolly socks and an extra jumper.
- Keep your hands and feet warm.
- Wear cool clothes in hot weather and drink water.
- Make a paper fan to cool you down, not a hand-held battery powered fan.

Wearing the right clothes can help to keep you at just the right temperature.

25%

35%

10%

15%

15%

The red areas show heat escaping from a house.

Ask your parents to make sure you have double-glazed windows fitted to keep the heat in.

Escaping air

In winter, warm air escapes from buildings into the cold air outside through cracks and holes and windows, making the heating work harder. There are all kinds of ways to fill in the gaps, stop warm air escaping and reduce carbon emissions.

Keep in the heat!

Adults can:
• Fill in cracks
• Put in double glazing
• Insulate lofts, walls and floors
• Keep furniture away from heating vents and radiators.
You can:
• Shut doors and windows
• Close curtains at night in the winter.

Action!

Make a snake draught excluder.

• You need an old stocking, knee-length sock or leg warmer longer than the bottom of your door.
• Stuff it with scraps of material so it is evenly filled.
• Tie the end. Give it eyes and a forked tongue.

Cooking and washing

Cooking food, keeping food cold, boiling the kettle and washing and drying clothes are things we do every day. They all use a great deal of energy, but there are lots of ways Green Team members can help to keep the bills down, save energy and reduce carbon emissions.

Washing

The most energy-efficient way of washing your clothes and dishes is in a machine on a low temperature cycle. Washing your clothes and dishes by hand in hot water uses more energy unless you do it very carefully. It saves energy to wait until the washing machine and dishwasher are full before you turn them on.

Drying

Clothes dryers use a lot of electricity. If you have one, putting on loads of washing one after the other makes the most of the heat already built up inside.

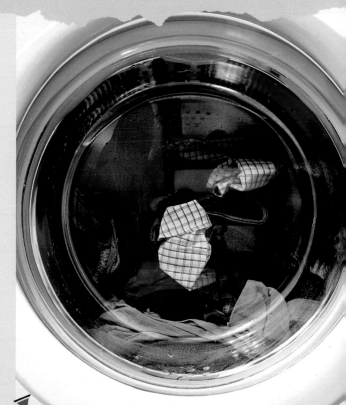

Make sure your washing machine is full before you turn it on, and only set it to 30 degrees Centigrade.

 ## Action!

Look at the care label on clothes before you buy them.

• Look out for those that can be washed on a cold cycle.

• Choose fabrics that need little or no ironing.

• Don't leave your clothes in a crumpled heap on the floor!

• Hang wet clothes on a washing line or rack, rather than putting them in a tumble drier.

Some dishwashers have an "air-dry" setting. That means no extra heat is used to dry the dishes.

Ironing

An iron uses lots of energy. You can dry clothes on a hanger instead to save creasing, and smooth t-shirts with your hands and fold them carefully so they don't need ironing.

Briquettes produced by crop waste are used to power the new energy-saving stove.

Children enjoy chapattis cooked on one of Ramesh Nibhoria's cookstoves.

Cooking

We all use a lot of energy when we cook food to eat. Most stoves run on fossil fuels such as gas or electricity produced from burning coal. There are lots of ways to reduce the energy used in cooking (see Challenge panel). It is also possible to cook on stoves that use renewable, or greener energy, however.

Case study – Cooking in the Punjab, India

In the Punjab, in India, schools cook their food on stoves run on fossil fuel. An alternative is to run stoves on fuel called biomass briquettes but existing stoves are not adapted for the use of briquettes. Ramesh Nibhoria, a local engineer and entrepreneur, has come up with a solution to this problem. He has developed the Sanja Chulha, which is specially designed to run on briquettes made from crop waste left over from the harvest.

Benefits for everybody

As the crop waste is a renewable source of energy, replacing a fossil fuel, the new stoves cut CO_2 emissions whilst reducing schools' fuel bills. Local farmers, who can now sell their waste to the briquette makers, also benefit from a new source of income.

Challenge!

You can save energy by taking a few simple steps when you cook.

• Putting the lid on a saucepan keeps in the heat and cooks more efficiently. Without a lid, 3 times more energy is used!
• Use pots made of heavy and thick material that keep in the heat.

! 1 biofuel school stove = 39 tonnes of CO_2 saved per year

Carbon offsetting

The aim of carbon offsetting is to keep the amount of carbon in the atmosphere the same, and not add to it. The way it is done is by balancing the amount of carbon emissions created by one action with another action that reduces the amount of carbon dioxide in the air.

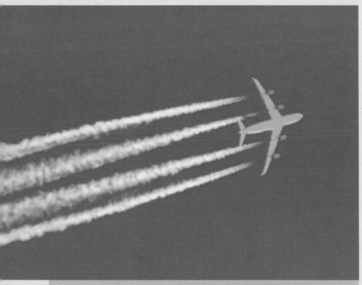

Aeroplanes release carbon dioxide high in the atmosphere.

Trees take in carbon dioxide in the air and give out oxygen, which we breathe in.

How it works

Step 1 is to work out how much carbon we put into the air when we do something that uses energy, such as taking a flight to go on holiday.

Step 2 is to do something that reduces the same amount of carbon in the air, for example, planting a tree or reducing the number of trips we make by car or bus.

Case study – Climate Care

Climate Care is an organisation that offsets carbon emissions by funding projects around the world. For example, you can work out the carbon emissions of your family car for a year, and Climate Care will tell you how much offsetting that amount of carbon will cost. They put your money towards a project that uses renewable energy, helps people to reduce their fuel consumption or replants forests.

Climate Care Carbon Calculator

- Return flight between New York and London – 9,656 kilometres
- Amount of carbon put into the atmosphere – 1.5 tonnes CO_2
- Cost of carbon offsetting – £11.55

A worker plants trees in a reforestation area in western Washington, USA.

Nelson Mandela and members of ELI, with one of the company's energy efficient light bulbs.

Climate Care offsetting projects – Reforestation

Cutting down trees means an increase in carbon dioxide as it reduces the number of plants that are able to convert this greenhouse gas into oxygen. Money paid to offset your carbon emissions could go towards replanting forests.

Reducing electricity use

Reducing our use of energy is an important way of reducing carbon emissions, but doing this can be expensive. The Efficient Lighting Initiative (ELI) works in developing countries to promote energy saving.

Most of the electricity in South Africa is made in coal-fired power stations which have high carbon emissions. To help reduce electricity use, ELI is installing energy-efficient lighting where people could not afford it themselves.

Challenge!

Find a carbon calculator on the Internet.

Ask an adult to help you work out the carbon emissions for your family.

Action!

Choose one thing at school that produces carbon emissions and take action.

• Plan ways to reduce the school's use of electricity.

• When you have done this, calculate the carbon emissions and choose how your school would like to offset the emissions.

Transport

Getting around uses energy. When you walk or cycle, you use your own energy. Cars use petrol and diesel for fuel, aeroplanes use aviation fuel and ferries and ships need fuel too. Members of the Green Team find ways to cut back on burning fuel when they travel.

Travelling by bus rather than by car helps to cut down on carbon emissions.

Heavy traffic in Beijing, China, causes air pollution. It makes people ill and makes global warming worse. People are being encouraged to cycle instead.

Public transport

Travelling by public transport, such as by bus, train or tram, means one big vehicle carrying lots of people at a time instead of lots of small vehicles carrying a few people at a time. Fewer vehicles mean less energy is used.

Travelling by bike

Cycling to work or school is the greenest way to travel. Bikes release no greenhouse gases at all.

Challenge!

Choose a journey that you often make by car, for example going to school or to the shops.

• Find out how you could get there on public transport.

• Try to do about one in three of those journeys on public transport in future.

Cheap flights make it possible for people to travel around the world on holiday.

Flying

Flying has made the world a smaller place because people can travel around the world quickly and cheaply on holiday and on business. But flying adds to carbon emissions in the air. More and more flights are planned which will add to the problem.

Going on holiday

Going on holiday usually involves travelling by car, coach, boat, train or plane. You can choose to calculate the carbon emissions of your journey and offset them (see pages 22-23). You can also choose a holiday that doesn't involve long journeys in vehicles that burn fuel.

Action!

Plan a holiday week at home for all the family that involves very little travel.

- Do something special every day.
- Go to interesting places nearby, for example a nature reserve or museum.
- Work out how to get there on public transport.
- Plan a circular walk starting and ending at home.
- Pack a picnic and enjoy being outside all day.
- Enjoy your local park, swimming pool and tennis courts.

This family travelled by bus to get here. They are supporting their local nature reserve and having a good day out.

Going to school

In the morning and in the mid-afternoon, the roads get very busy as children are taken to school and collected by car. Green Team members try to reduce the fuel they burn getting to school by sharing lifts, travelling on public transport, the school bus, cycling or walking.

Cycling to school is a great way to save energy and also to get fit.

Saving energy

To reduce the number of school journeys, some families take it in turns to drive their own children and other people's to school. Others encourage their children to walk or cycle to school.

Challenge!

If you can't ride a bike, learn how to.

• If you haven't got a bike ask if you can borrow a friend's, and try it out.

• Encourage your mum and dad to cycle with you.

• Wear a helmet and find safe places to ride.

• Take a cycling proficiency course.

Case study – Sustrans Bike It!

Sustrans is short for sustainable transport. This group runs a scheme called Bike It, which encourages children to cycle to school. A Sustrans Bike It officer works with 12 schools, explaining the benefits of cycling and organising events and activities to motivate and inspire more children to cycle to school.

Louise, 12, says:

"Bike It is a good thing because it is more refreshing cycling than going in a car. I think it is important to stop pollution further, and cycling helps the environment."

These children are taking a "walking bus" to school in Hertfordshire, England. They are walking together, forming a human "bus".

Walking buses are used all over the world. Here, children are walking to school on the island of Funafuti in Polynesia.

iwalk

International Walk to School Month

Case study – Walk to School

International Walk to School month is an annual event to raise worldwide awareness of walking issues. Pupils everywhere can join in with children all over the world and walk to school for a month.

The walks promote:
- Physical activity
- Road awareness
- Awareness of how walkable a community is and where improvements can be made
- Concern for the environment
- Reducing traffic congestion, pollution and traffic speed near schools
- Taking back neighbourhoods for people on foot.

Action!

Get involved with Walk to School Month and then make walking to school a habit.

Glossary

Carbon emissions
Carbon emissions are the carbon that is sent into the atmosphere when we burn fuels such as coal, oil and gas for energy.

Carbon offset
To carbon offset is to balance the amount of carbon put into the atmosphere with an action that reduces carbon in the atmosphere so that the amount of carbon is not increased.

Energy efficient
To be energy efficient is to use energy in a way that is not wasteful, for example by insulating a house to stop heat from escaping.

Insulate
To insulate a building is to protect it from heat escaping or cold air getting in, for example, by putting in double glazing, filling in cracks and lining the loft with insulating material.

Nuclear energy
Nuclear energy is energy released when atoms are split up. Although it is a clean source of energy, it produces dangerous radioactive waste that has to be kept safe for thousands of years.

Renewable energy
Renewable energy is generated from something that can be replaced, such as biofuel from plants, or will never run out, such as wind, water and sunlight.

Standby
A machine on standby can be turned on by remote control. It is not completely turned off. A small light indicates it is still using energy and producing heat.

Sustainable
Something sustainable can be kept going. Using energy in a sustainable way means using it in a way that doesn't use it all up or destroy the environment.

Thermostat
A device that senses the temperature and keeps it at a steady level. A thermostat set at 18°C turns the central heating on or off to keep the temperature in the building as near as possible to 18°C.

Weblinks

www.iwalktoschool.org
Learn about International Walk to School Month and find out how you can join in with pupils all over the world and walk to school for a month.

www.sustrans.org.uk
Sustrans – short for sustainable transport – is an organisation that gets people to travel in a way that is healthy for them and for the environment.

www.jpmorganclimatecare.org
Climate Care offsets your CO_2 by funding renewable energy and energy efficiency projects around the world.

www.self.org
The Solar Electric Light Fund (SELF) is a non-profit charitable organisation that promotes, develops and facilitates solar rural electrification and energy SELF-sufficiency in developing countries.

www.eco-schools.org.uk
Your school can become part of an international group of schools committed to caring for the environment.

http://powerdown.actionaid.org.uk
Find out about Actionaid's Power Down initiative and how schools can lead the way and be part of the solution to climate change.

Note to parents and teachers:

Every effort has been made by the Publishers to ensure that these websites are suitable for children, that they are of the highest educational value, and that they contain no inappropriate or offensive material. However, because of the nature of the Internet, it is impossible to guarantee that the contents of these sites will not be altered. We strongly advise that Internet access is supervised by a responsible adult.

Index

TOWER HAMLETS

91 000 004 661 24 5

KU-863-048

Library Learning Information

To renew this item call:

0115 929 3388
or visit
www.ideastore.co.uk

TOWER HAMLETS

Created and managed by Tower Hamlets Council

OXFORD
UNIVERSITY PRESS

Great Clarendon Street, Oxford OX2 6DP

Oxford University Press is a department of the University of Oxford.
It furthers the University's objective of excellence in research,
scholarship, and education by publishing worldwide in

Oxford   New York

Auckland   Cape Town   Dar es Salaam   Hong Kong   Karachi
Kuala Lumpur   Madrid   Melbourne   Mexico City   Nairobi
New Delhi   Shanghai   Taipei   Toronto

With offices in

Argentina   Austria   Brazil   Chile   Czech Republic   France   Greece
Guatemala   Hungary   Italy   Japan   Poland   Portugal   Singapore
South Korea   Switzerland   Thailand   Turkey   Ukraine   Vietnam

Oxford is a registered trade mark of Oxford University Press in the UK and in certain other countries

© Oxford University Press 2015

All artwork by Dynamo Design Ltd. Developed with, and English text by, Jane Bingham and White-Thomson Publishing Ltd. Consultant David Burnie. Language project manager: Anna Stevenson. Contributors: David Burnie, Mary Rigby, Anne-Christine Titchener.

Database right Oxford University Press (maker)

First published 2015

All rights reserved. No part of this publication may be reproduced, stored in a retrieval system, or transmitted, in any form or by any means, without the prior permission in writing of Oxford University Press, or as expressly permitted by law, or under terms agreed with the appropriate reprographics rights organization. Enquiries concerning reproduction outside the scope of the above should be sent to the Rights Department, Oxford University Press, at the address above

You must not circulate this book in any other binding or cover and you must impose this same condition on any acquirer

British Library Cataloguing in Publication Data

Data available

ISBN 9780 19 273755 7

10 9 8 7 6 5 4 3 2 1

Printed in China

TOWER HAMLETS LIBRARIES	
91000004661245	
Bertrams	17/06/2015
J448.242	£10.99
THCUB	TH15000139

Oxford
FRENCH·ENGLISH
VISUAL
DICTIONARY OF
ANIMALS

OXFORD
UNIVERSITY PRESS

Sommaire

Contents

Comment utiliser ce dictionnaire

Ce dictionnaire est plein de mots sur les animaux, mais c'est aussi un livre d'information. Cela signifie que vous pouvez découvrir le monde naturel tout en apprenant de nouveaux mots !

This dictionary is packed with animal words, but it is also an information book. This means that you can find out about the natural world while you are learning new words!

Comment est-ce que j'utilise ce dictionnaire ?
How do I use the dictionary?

Le vocabulaire est présenté par des images, des mises-en-scène et des schémas. Cela vous permettra de trouver facilement le mot que vous recherchez tout en découvrant de nouveaux éléments de vocabulaire.

Words are introduced through pictures, scenes and labelled diagrams. This makes it easy to find the word you need – and discover more words along the way.

La barre d'en haut identifie le thème central.
Top bar identifies the topic section.

Les légendes vous en disent plus sur certains animaux.
Captions tell you more about certain animals.

L'introduction fournit des informations utiles supplémentaires.
Introduction provides useful extra information.

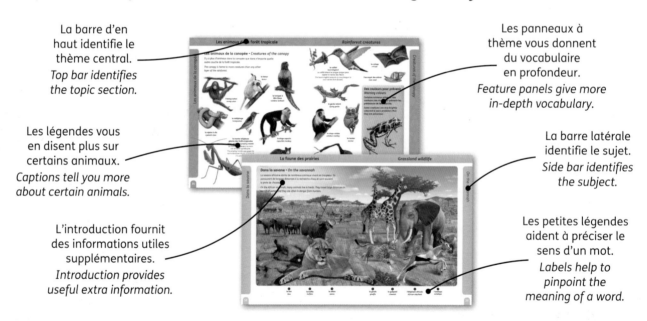

Les panneaux à thème vous donnent du vocabulaire en profondeur.
Feature panels give more in-depth vocabulary.

La barre latérale identifie le sujet.
Side bar identifies the subject.

Les petites légendes aident à préciser le sens d'un mot.
Labels help to pinpoint the meaning of a word.

Comment est-ce que je trouve un mot ? • *How do I find a word?*

Vous pouvez rechercher un mot de deux manières différentes. Vous pouvez consulter les thèmes du Sommaire. Ou vous pouvez utiliser l'index à la fin du livre. Il y a un index en anglais et un en français pour que vous puissiez trouver un mot dans l'une ou l'autre des deux langues.

There are two ways to search for a word. You can look through the topics on the Contents page. Or you can use the Index at the back of the book. There is an English index and a French one, so you can find a word in either language.

Comment est-il organisé ? • *How is it organized?*

pages 10-13
La vie et le comportement des animaux
Animal life and behaviour

Cette section décrit les animaux et comment ils vivent.

Looks at animals and how they live.

pages 14-27
Des animaux de toutes sortes • *All kinds of animals*

Cette section présente les six principaux groupes d'animaux : les mammifères ;
les oiseaux ; les reptiles ; les amphibiens ; les poissons et autres créatures
marines ; les insectes et les petites bêtes.

*Covers the six main animal groups: Mammals; Birds; Reptiles; Amphibians;
Fish and other sea creatures; and Insects and minibeasts.*

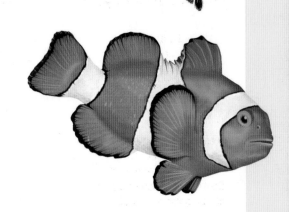

pages 28-105
L'habitat des animaux • *Animal habitats*

Cette section présente les animaux dans leur habitat naturel,
comme les forêts tropicales, les montagnes et les déserts.

*Introduces animals in their natural habitats, such as rainforests,
mountains and deserts.*

pages 106-109
Les animaux et les oiseaux très répandus
Widespread creatures and birds

Cette section présente des créatures que l'on trouve dans un
grand éventail d'habitats à travers le monde.

Shows creatures that are found in a wide range of habitats across the world.

pages 110-113
Des mots sur les animaux • *Animal words*

Cette section explique le vocabulaire pour les jeunes, ainsi que pour
les groupes d'animaux et les bruits.

Gives words for young animals, and for animal groups and sounds.

pages 114-115
Le quiz des animaux • *Animal detective quiz*

Il vous permet de tester vos connaissances sur les animaux !

Offers you the chance to test your animal knowledge!

Quelques règles de grammaire et de prononciation

This book is for people learning their first words in French. By looking at the pictures you can learn the words for a whole range of themes.

Most of the words in this book are nouns, but some are verbs and some are adjectives. Nouns are words that give names to things, people or places. For example, *grenouille* (frog), *cheval* (horse) and *oiseau* (bird) are all nouns. Verbs are doing words; they refer to actions. For example, **chasser** (hunt), **vivre** (live) and **voler** (fly) are all verbs.

Most nouns are either masculine or feminine in French. We call this gender, and this is shown in this book by putting the word for 'the' before the noun: *le* (masculine) or *la* (feminine).

When a noun begins with a vowel (a, e, i, o, u), and with many that begin with 'h', *le* or *la* becomes *l'* – for example *l'hirondelle* (swallow), *l'hôtel* (hotel). The index will show you whether these words are masculine or feminine. Note that there is no space between l' and the noun.

> **TIP:** When you learn a new word, always try to learn whether it is masculine or feminine.

We say that a noun is 'plural' when it refers to two or more things. With plural nouns, the word for 'the' is *les*: *les rivières* (rivers), *les branchies* (gills).

Adjectives are words that describe nouns; for example *grand* (big), *petit* (small). Many adjectives have a different form for masculine and feminine: often you just add an extra 'e' to make the feminine adjective from the masculine form; compare *le désert chaud* (hot desert) with *la région chaude* (hot region). On the other hand, if an adjective already ends in an 'e', you don't add another 'e': *le courant rapide* (fast current), *la chasse rapide* (fast hunt).

Some words for animals have different forms depending on whether you're talking about a male animal or a female animal: *le chat* (male), *la chatte* (female).

Pronunciation

Single letters

c (+ a, o, u): – 'k': *cabillaud, cou, locuste*

c (+ e, i) – 's': *cerf, cigale*

g (+ u, a) – like 'g' in 'gun': *guêpe, gazelle*

g (+ e, i) – like the second 'g' in 'garage': *nageoire, géant*

h – is silent at the beginning of a word: *l'herbe, le homard, la hulotte*

j – sounds like the soft 'j' in 'pleasure': *jambe*

r – sounds like clearing your throat or gargling: *rat, oreille*

u – round your lips as if you're going to say 'oo' but try to make an 'ee' sound instead, without changing the shape of your lips: *tortue, museau*

x – is silent at the end of a word: *chevaux, creux*

Groups of letters

ch – like 'sh' in English: *cheval, poche*

eau – 'oh': *oiseau*

en – say 'on' through your nose: *dent*

eu – 'euh': *queue*

in – say 'an' through your nose: *pince*

gn – silent 'g'; sounds like 'ny': *araignée*

ll – sometimes pronounced with a 'y' sound: *oreille;* **sometimes like 'l':** *femelle*

œ – 'eur', like 'learn': *cœur*

ou – 'ooh': *rouge*

oi – 'wah': *proie*

th – the 'h' is silent: *panthère*

ui – 'oo-ee': *nuit, truite*

Accents

à – like the 'a' in 'back'

ç – 's': *français*

é – 'ay': *éléphant*

è – like the English 'air': *lièvre*

ê – similar to è: *forêt*

La vie des animaux

Il y a des millions d'espèces animales sur Terre, d'une diversité de tailles et de formes étonnantes.

There are millions of species of animals on Earth and they come in an amazing range of shapes and sizes!

Les vertébrés et les invertébrés • *Vertebrates and invertebrates*

Les animaux peuvent être des vertébrés ou des invertébrés. Les vertébrés possèdent une colonne vertébrale (ou une épine dorsale). Les invertébrés n'ont pas de colonne vertébrale.

Animals can be vertebrates or invertebrates. Vertebrates have a spine (or backbone). Invertebrates do not have a spine.

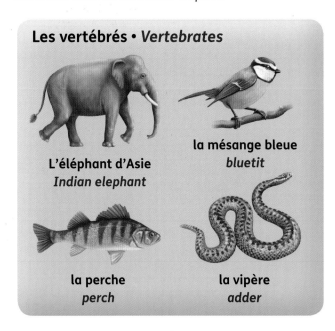

Les vertébrés • *Vertebrates*

L'éléphant d'Asie
Indian elephant

la mésange bleue
bluetit

la perche
perch

la vipère
adder

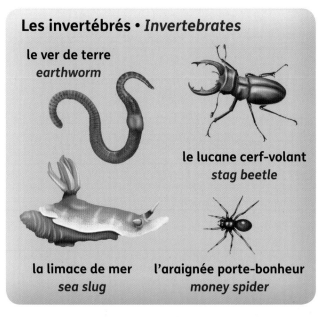

Les invertébrés • *Invertebrates*

le ver de terre
earthworm

le lucane cerf-volant
stag beetle

la limace de mer
sea slug

l'araignée porte-bonheur
money spider

Se déplacer et manger • *Moving and eating*

Les animaux sont différents des autres formes de vie comme les plantes et les champignons, parce qu'ils sont mobiles et survivent en mangeant d'autres formes de vie.

Animals are different from other living things, such as plants and fungi, because they are more mobile and they survive by eating other life forms.

Les moutons broutent l'herbe. Les animaux qui se nourrissent exclusivement de plantes sont appelés des herbivores.
Sheep graze on grass. Creatures that eat only plants are called herbivores.

Les tigres chassent et tuent leur proie. Les mangeurs de viande sont appelés des carnivores.
Tigers hunt and kill their prey. Meat-eaters are called carnivores.

Les parasites • *Parasites*

Les parasites se nourrissent des corps d'autres animaux.

Parasites feed off the body of another animal.

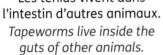

Les sangsues sucent
le sang d'animaux
plus grands.
*Leeches suck blood
from larger creatures.*

Les ténias vivent dans
l'intestin d'autres animaux.
*Tapeworms live inside the
guts of other animals.*

Les puces vivent dans
les poils des mammifères
et des oiseaux.
*Fleas live in the coats of
mammals and birds.*

Les sens des animaux • *Animal senses*

Les animaux utilisent la vue, l'ouïe, l'odorat
et le toucher pour les aider à trouver de la
nourriture et rester en dehors du danger.

*Animals use sight, hearing, smell and touch
to help them find food and stay safe.*

Les hiboux possèdent de
grands yeux qui laissent entrer
beaucoup de lumière. Ceci leur
permet de chasser la nuit.
*Owls have large eyes that let
in a lot of light so they can
hunt at night.*

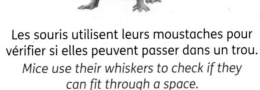

Les souris utilisent leurs moustaches pour
vérifier si elles peuvent passer dans un trou.
*Mice use their whiskers to check if they
can fit through a space.*

Le puissant sens de l'odorat du loup lui
permet de suivre l'odeur d'un animal.
*A wolf's powerful sense of smell allows it
to track an animal's scent.*

Les lapins utilisent leurs longues
oreilles souples pour rester à l'affût
du danger autour d'eux.
*Rabbits use their long, flexible ears to
listen out for danger from all sides.*

Le comportement animal

Les zoologistes observent les animaux de près et étudient leur comportement. Ces deux pages traitent de la parade de séduction, des affrontements, de la migration et de l'hibernation des animaux.

Zoologists observe animals closely and study their behaviour. These two pages cover courtship, fighting, migration and hibernation.

La parade de séduction • *Courtship*

La plupart des animaux ont besoin de trouver un partenaire pour créer une nouvelle vie. Les mâles ont recours à divers comportements de séduction pour attirer leur compagne.

Most creatures need to find a mate to create new life. Males use a range of courtship behaviour to attract a mate.

L'oiseau de tonnelle rassemble des objets colores.
The bowerbird collects colourful objects.

Le crabe violoniste agite son énorme pince.
The fiddler crab waves its enormous claw.

Les rainettes coassent de façon bruyante et saccadée.
Tree frogs make repeated loud croaks.

L'oiseau de paradis affiche son plumage.
The bird of paradise displays its plumage.

Les affrontements • *Fighting*

Les mâles doivent souvent repousser des rivaux avant de conquérir la femelle.
Males often have to fight off rivals before they can win their mate.

Les cerfs luttent avec leurs bois.
Stags lock antlers to fight.

Les serpents à sonnette essaient de se pousser à terre.
Rattlesnakes try to push each other to the ground.

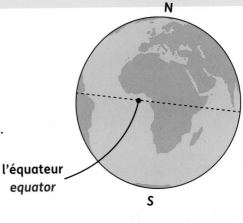

l'équateur
equator

La migration • *Migration*

Certains animaux font de très longs trajets pour se reproduire ou trouver de la nourriture. C'est ce qu'on appelle la migration.

Some animals make very long journeys to breed or find food. This is called migration.

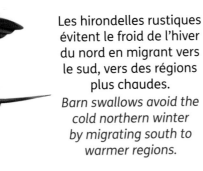

Les hirondelles rustiques évitent le froid de l'hiver du nord en migrant vers le sud, vers des régions plus chaudes.
Barn swallows avoid the cold northern winter by migrating south to warmer regions.

Les saumons de l'Atlantique naissent dans les rivières, migrent vers l'océan, puis reviennent à la rivière où ils sont nés pour se reproduire.
Atlantic salmon are born in rivers, migrate to the ocean and then return to the same river to breed.

Les baleines à bosse mettent bas près de l'équateur, mais elles se nourrissent principalement dans les mers polaires.
Humpback whales give birth near the equator, but their main feeding grounds are in the polar seas.

Les animaux qui hibernent • *Hibernating creatures*

la chauve-souris pipistrelle
pipistrelle bat

Pendant les mois froids de l'hiver, certains animaux hibernent. Ils sombrent dans un sommeil très profond et toutes leurs fonctions corporelles ralentissent.

In the cold winter months some animals hibernate. They sink into a very deep sleep and all their body functions slow down.

le hamster
hamster

la tortue-boîte
box turtle

le bourdon
bumblebee

13

Il existe un éventail incroyable de créatures vivant sur Terre. Découvrez les principaux groupes d'animaux ici.

There is an amazing range of creatures living on Earth. Find out about the main animal groups here.

Les mammifères • *Mammals*

Les mammifères comprennent les lions, les chauves-souris et les baleines – et, bien sûr, les êtres humains ! Ils ont le sang chaud, et de la fourrure ou des poils sur le corps. Toutes les mères de ce groupe d'animaux produisent du lait pour nourrir leurs petits.

Mammals include lions, bats and whales – and, of course, human beings! They are warm-blooded and have fur or body hair. All mammal mothers produce milk to feed their young.

Le cheval
Horse

la crinière
mane

la narine
nostril

la croupe
croup

la patte avant
foreleg

la patte arrière
hind leg

le flanc
flank

la poitrine
barrel

le sabot
hoof

le boulet
fetlock

l'oreille
ear

l'œil
eye

la queue
tail

le museau
muzzle

le dos
back

les dents
teeth

Le chien
Dog

la langue
tongue

la griffe
claw

la patte
paw

le doigt
finger

le pouce
thumb

le bras
arm

Le singe
Monkey

la poitrine
chest

le pied
foot

l'orteil
toe

la jambe
leg

Les organes internes d'un grand singe
Internal organs of an ape

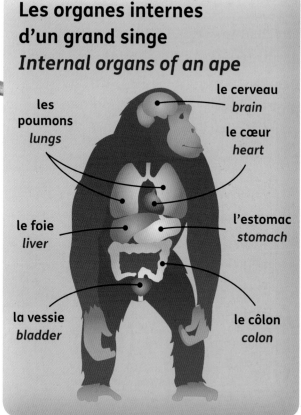

les poumons
lungs

le cerveau
brain

le cœur
heart

le foie
liver

l'estomac
stomach

la vessie
bladder

le côlon
colon

Les marsupiaux
Marsupials

Les marsupiaux sont un groupe de mammifères que l'on trouve principalement en Australie. Les mères portent leurs bébés dans une poche jusqu'à ce qu'ils soient assez grands pour survivre seuls.

Marsupials are a group of mammals found mainly in Australia. The mothers carry their babies in a pouch until the babies are old enough to survive on their own.

Le kangourou
Kangaroo

le bébé
baby

la mamelle
teat

la poche
pouch

Le bébé tète le lait des mamelles de sa mère. *The baby suckles milk from its mother's teats.*

Les oiseaux • *Birds*

Les oiseaux ont le sang chaud et sont recouverts de plumes. Tous les oiseaux pondent des œufs et la plupart d'entre eux peuvent voler, mais il y en a, tels que l'autruche, qui ne le peuvent pas.

Birds are warm-blooded and covered with feathers. All birds lay eggs and most of them can fly, but there are some large flightless birds, like the ostrich.

le bout de l'aile
wingtip

l'aile
wing

le bec
beak

L'aigle
Eagle

les serres
talons

la queue
tail

Les plumes • *Feathers*

La plupart des oiseaux ont trois sortes de plumes, et chaque sorte a une fonction importante.

Most birds have three types of feather and each type has an important function.

Les plumes de duvet maintiennent la chaleur corporelle de l'oiseau.
Down feathers keep the bird's body warm.

Les plumes de couverture donnent une forme profilée à l'oiseau.
Body feathers give the bird a streamlined shape.

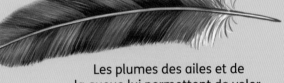

Les plumes des ailes et de la queue lui permettent de voler.
The wing and tail feathers allow it to fly.

Différents becs • *Different bills*

Il existe différentes formes de becs adaptés à différents modes d'alimentation.

There are different shapes of bills (or beaks) for different ways of feeding.

Les échassiers attrapent des poissons sous l'eau.
Waders grab fish underwater.

Les oiseaux de proie déchirent la chair de leur proie.
Birds of prey tear up their food.

Les perroquets craquent la coquille des noix pour les vider.
Parrots crack and shell nuts.

L'oie
Goose

le cou
neck

le bec
bill

la poitrine
breast

les pattes palmées
webbed feet

Les canards ramassent de la nourriture à surface de l'eau.
Ducks scoop up food from the water's surface.

Les reptiles • *Reptiles*

Les reptiles ont une peau résistante, sèche et écailleuse. Tous les reptiles sont des animaux à sang froid, ils ont donc besoin de se réchauffer au soleil.

Reptiles have a tough, dry skin that is covered with scales. All reptiles are cold-blooded, so they need to bask in the sun to warm up.

la narine
nostril

le museau
snout

Le crocodile
Crocodile

la peau
écailleuse
scaly skin

la mâchoire
jaw

les griffes
claws

la nageoire
flipper

La tortue marine
Turtle

la carapace
shell

le dessous
du ventre
underbelly

Le camouflage • *Camouflage*

De nombreux animaux se camouflent pour se fondre dans leur environnement.

Many animals use camouflage to blend in with their surroundings.

le python birman
Burmese python

la tortue d'Hermann
Hermann's tortoise

le dragon d'eau chinois
Chinese water dragon lizard

Le serpent
Snake

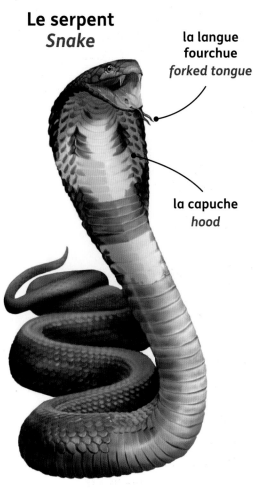

la langue fourchue
forked tongue

la capuche
hood

Le venin • *Venom*

Certains serpents et lézards injectent dans leurs proies un poison appelé venin. Leur venin peut paralyser ou même tuer la victime.

Some snakes and lizards inject a poison called venom into their prey. Their venom can paralyse or even kill a victim.

La vipère
Viper

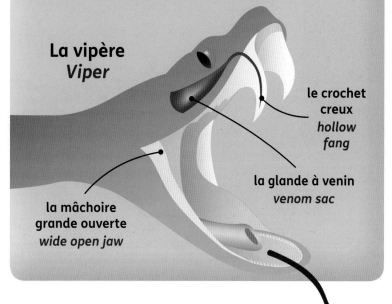

le crochet creux
hollow fang

la glande à venin
venom sac

la mâchoire grande ouverte
wide open jaw

Les amphibiens • *Amphibians*

Les amphibiens ont la peau lisse et sont à sang froid. Ils éclosent et se développent habituellement dans l'eau, mais passent le plus clair de leur vie sur la terre. Grenouilles, crapauds, salamandres et tritons sont tous des amphibiens.

Amphibians have smooth skin and are cold-blooded. They usually hatch and develop in water, but then spend most of their adult lives on land. Frogs, toads, salamanders and newts are all amphibians.

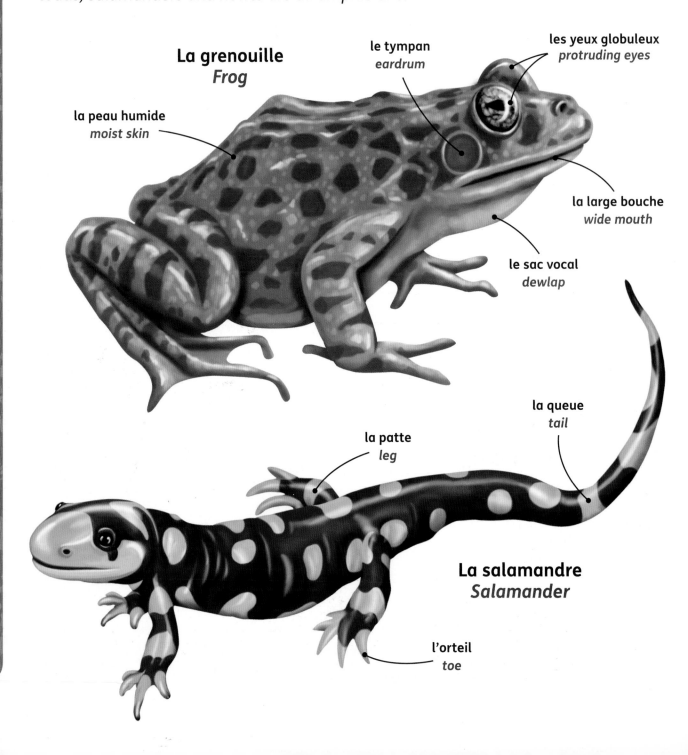

La grenouille
Frog

le tympan
eardrum

les yeux globuleux
protruding eyes

la peau humide
moist skin

la large bouche
wide mouth

le sac vocal
dewlap

la queue
tail

la patte
leg

La salamandre
Salamander

l'orteil
toe

Le cycle de vie de la grenouille
Lifecycle of a frog

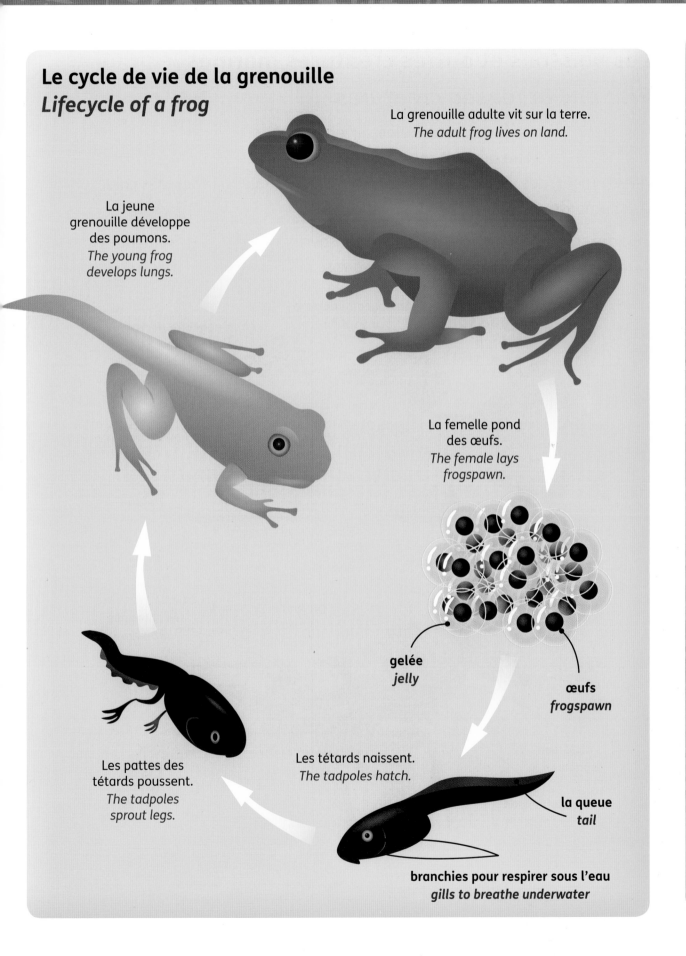

La grenouille adulte vit sur la terre.
The adult frog lives on land.

La jeune grenouille développe des poumons.
The young frog develops lungs.

La femelle pond des œufs.
The female lays frogspawn.

gelée
jelly

œufs
frogspawn

Les tétards naissent.
The tadpoles hatch.

Les pattes des tétards poussent.
The tadpoles sprout legs.

la queue
tail

branchies pour respirer sous l'eau
gills to breathe underwater

Les poissons et autres créatures marines
Fish and other sea creatures

Les poissons possèdent une colonne vertébrale, et sont spécialement adaptée pour leur permettre de vivre sous l'eau. Parmi les créatures de la mer, on trouve des éponges, des vers marins, des méduses, des étoiles de mer, des calamars et des homards.

Fish are creatures with backbones and are specially adapted to live underwater. Other sea creatures include sponges, worms, jellyfish, starfish, squid and lobsters.

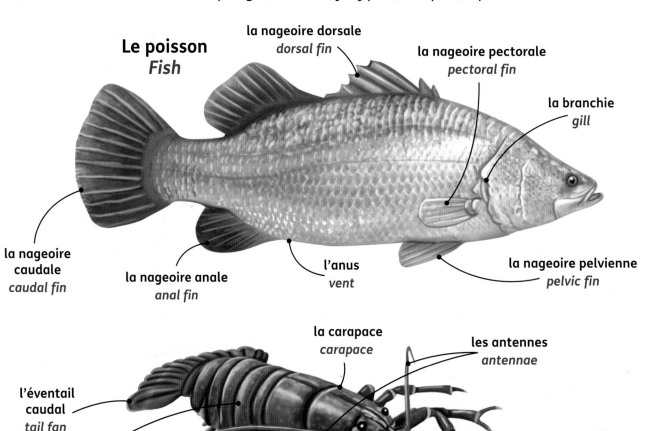

Le poisson
Fish

la nageoire dorsale
dorsal fin

la nageoire pectorale
pectoral fin

la branchie
gill

la nageoire caudale
caudal fin

la nageoire anale
anal fin

l'anus
vent

la nageoire pelvienne
pelvic fin

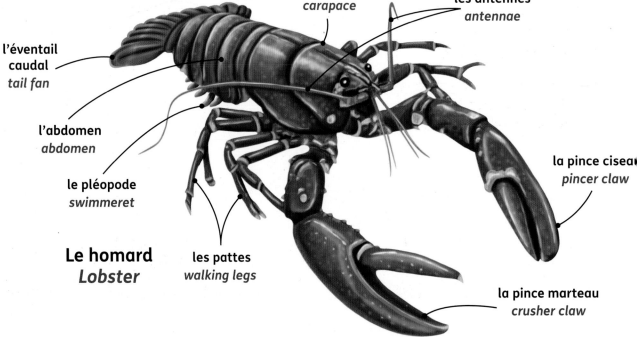

la carapace
carapace

les antennes
antennae

l'éventail caudal
tail fan

l'abdomen
abdomen

le pléopode
swimmeret

Le homard
Lobster

les pattes
walking legs

la pince ciseau
pincer claw

la pince marteau
crusher claw

All kinds of animals

la tête
head

l'œil
eye

le bec
beak

le siphon
siphon

la tentacule
arm

la ventouse
sucker

La pieuvre
Octopus

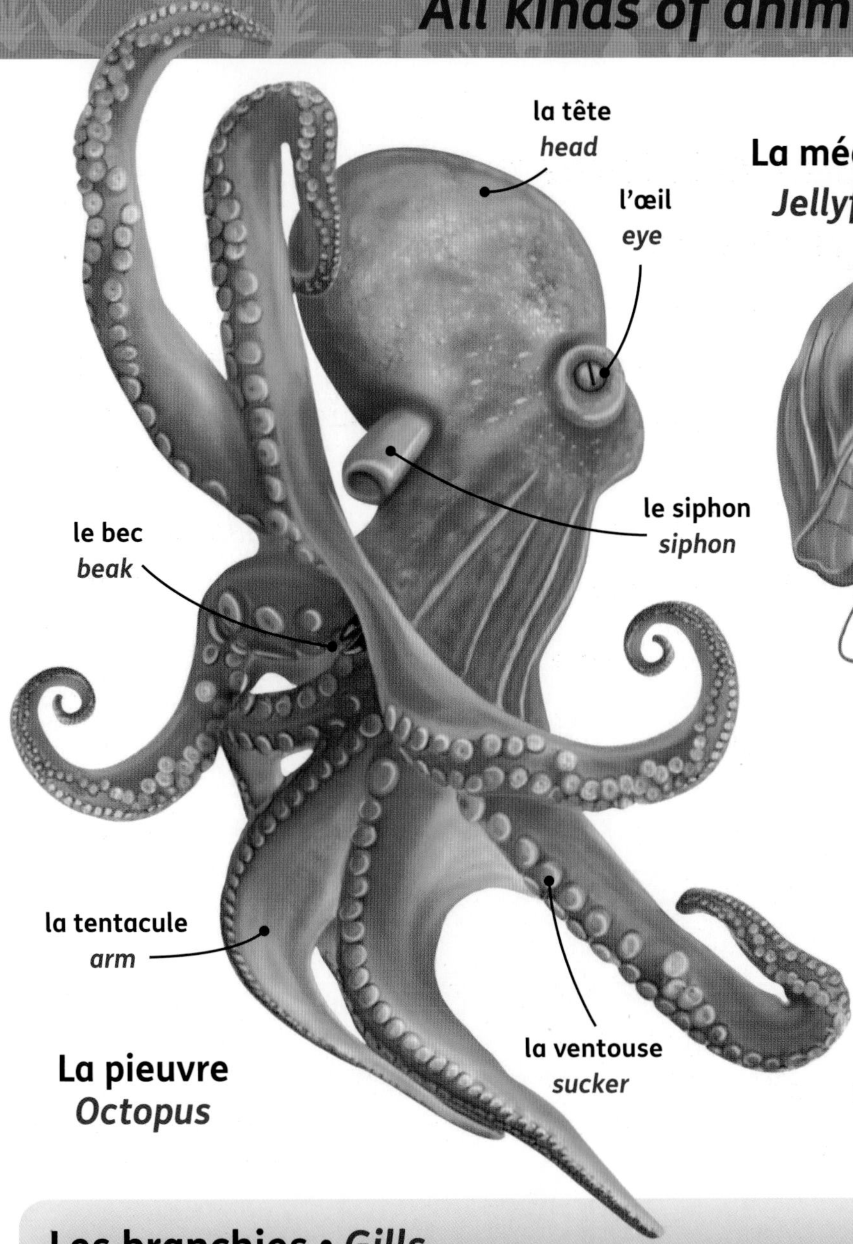

La méduse
Jellyfish

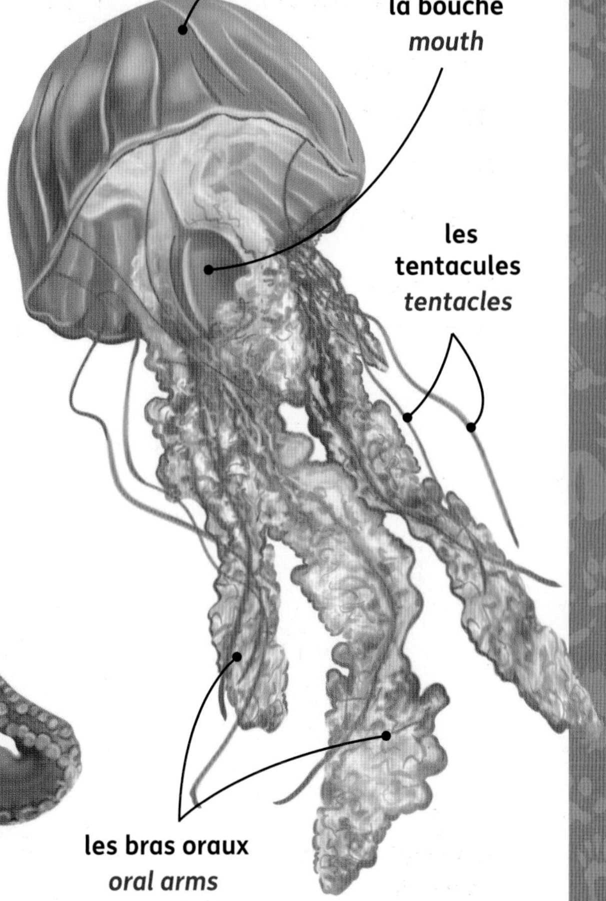

l'ombrelle
bell

la bouche
mouth

les tentacules
tentacles

les bras oraux
oral arms

Les branchies • *Gills*

Les poissons utilisent leurs branchies pour respirer l'oxygène dissout dans l'eau.

Fish use their gills to breathe the oxygen dissolved in water.

Les branchies extraient l'oxygène de l'eau.
The gills extract oxygen from the water.

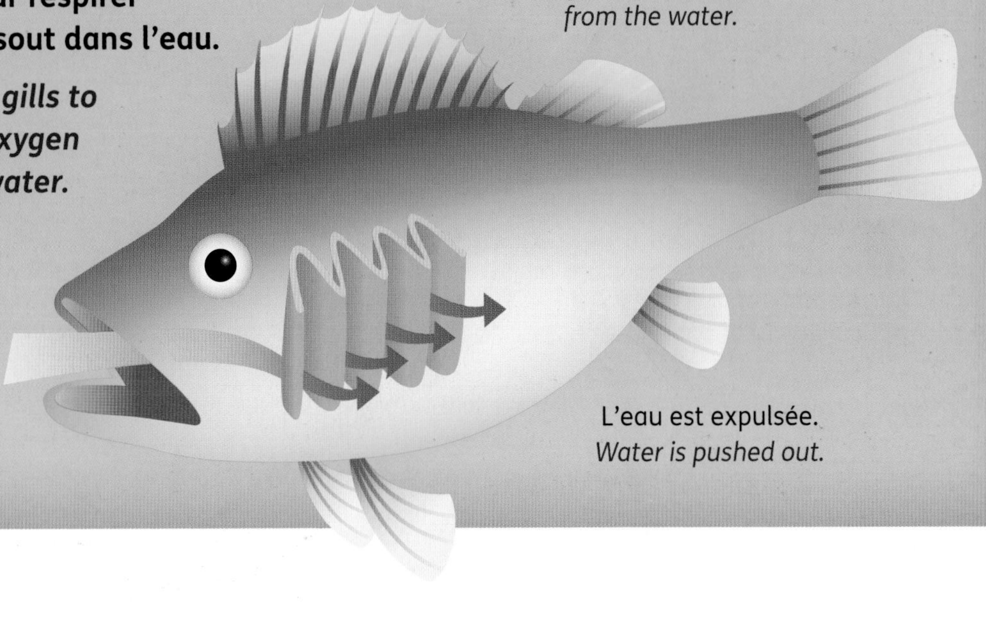

L'eau est aspirée.
Water is sucked in.

L'eau est expulsée.
Water is pushed out.

25

Les insectes et les petites bêtes
Insects and minibeasts

Les insectes ont un corps composé de trois parties : la tête, le thorax et l'abdomen. Ils possèdent tous six pattes, et certains ont des ailes. Les insectes comprennent les scarabées, les papillons et les abeilles. Parmi les petites bêtes, on trouve les araignées, les mille-pattes et les cloportes.

Insects have bodies with three parts: the head, the thorax and the abdomen. All insects have six legs, and some have wings. Insects include beetles, butterflies and bees. Minibeasts include spiders, centipedes and woodlice.

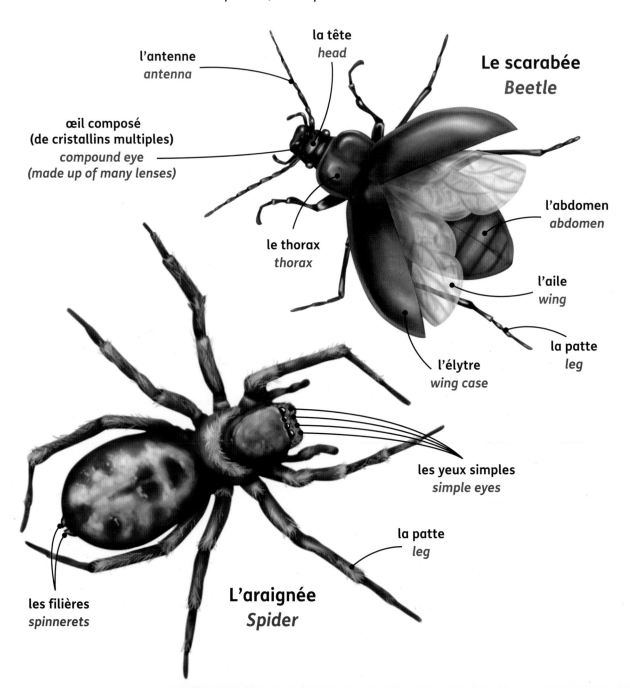

la tête
head

l'antenne
antenna

œil composé
(de cristallins multiples)
*compound eye
(made up of many lenses)*

Le scarabée
Beetle

l'abdomen
abdomen

le thorax
thorax

l'aile
wing

la patte
leg

l'élytre
wing case

les yeux simples
simple eyes

la patte
leg

les filières
spinnerets

L'araignée
Spider

L'abeille • *Honey bee*

L'abeille recueille le nectar à l'intérieur des fleurs et propage le pollen d'une fleur à l'autre.
The honey bee collects nectar from inside flowers and spreads pollen from one flower to another.

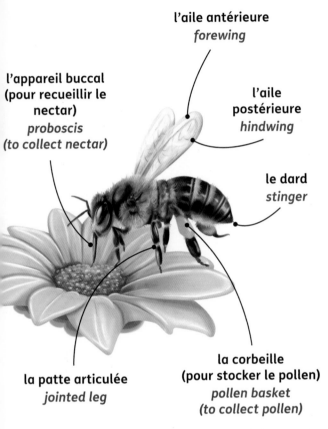

l'aile antérieure
forewing

l'appareil buccal (pour recueillir le nectar)
proboscis (to collect nectar)

l'aile postérieure
hindwing

le dard
stinger

la patte articulée
jointed leg

la corbeille (pour stocker le pollen)
pollen basket (to collect pollen)

Les ruches • *Beehives*

À l'intérieur d'une ruche, on trouve une reine, des centaines de faux-bourdons et des milliers d'ouvrières.

A hive contains one queen bee, hundreds of drones and thousands of workers.

la reine • *queen*
La reine pond des œufs pour produire plus d'abeilles.
The queen lays eggs to produce more bees.

le faux-bourdon • *drone*
Les faux-bourdons s'accouplent avec la reine pour créer de nouvelles ruches.
Drones mate with the queen to start new hives.

l'ouvrière • *worker*
Les ouvrières s'occupent des jeunes et produisent du miel.
Workers look after the young and make honey.

Le cycle de vie d'un papillon
Lifecycle of a butterfly

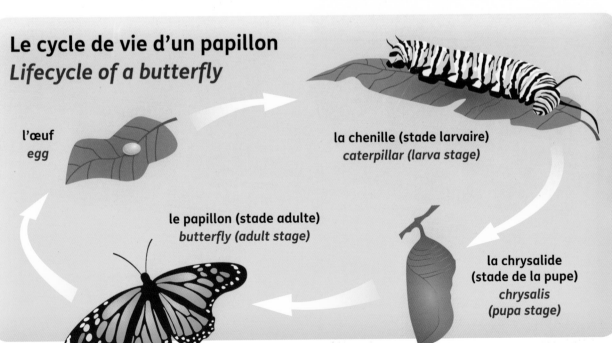

l'œuf
egg

la chenille (stade larvaire)
caterpillar (larva stage)

le papillon (stade adulte)
butterfly (adult stage)

la chrysalide (stade de la pupe)
chrysalis (pupa stage)

À l'intérieur de la forêt tropicale il fait chaud et humide
et il y a beaucoup de bruits...

Inside the rainforest it is hot and steamy and very noisy...

LES ANIMAUX DE LA FORÊT TROPICALE
RAINFOREST CREATURES

Les habitats de la forêt tropicale • *Rainforest habitats*

La majorité des forêts tropicales sont caractéristiques des régions tropicales. Elles poussent près de l'équateur où il fait chaud et humide. Les forêts tempérées se situent dans les régions moins chaudes du monde.

Most rainforests are tropical. They grow close to the equator, where it is hot and rainy. Temperate rainforests are found in cooler parts of the world.

Les couches de la forêt tropicale • *Rainforest layers*

La forêt tropicale a quatre couches principales. Chacune de ces couches accueille différents animaux, bien que certains se déplacent d'une couche à l'autre.

Rainforests have four main layers. Each one is home to different animals, although some creatures move between the layers.

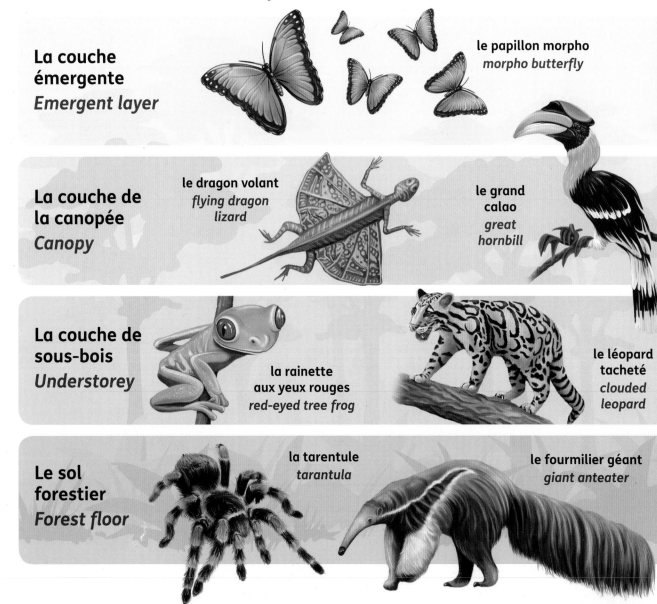

La couche émergente
Emergent layer

le papillon morpho
morpho butterfly

La couche de la canopée
Canopy

le dragon volant
flying dragon lizard

le grand calao
great hornbill

La couche de sous-bois
Understorey

la rainette aux yeux rouges
red-eyed tree frog

le léopard tacheté
clouded leopard

Le sol forestier
Forest floor

la tarentule
tarantula

le fourmilier géant
giant anteater

Rainforest creatures

Principales régions de forêts tropicales • *Major rainforest regions*

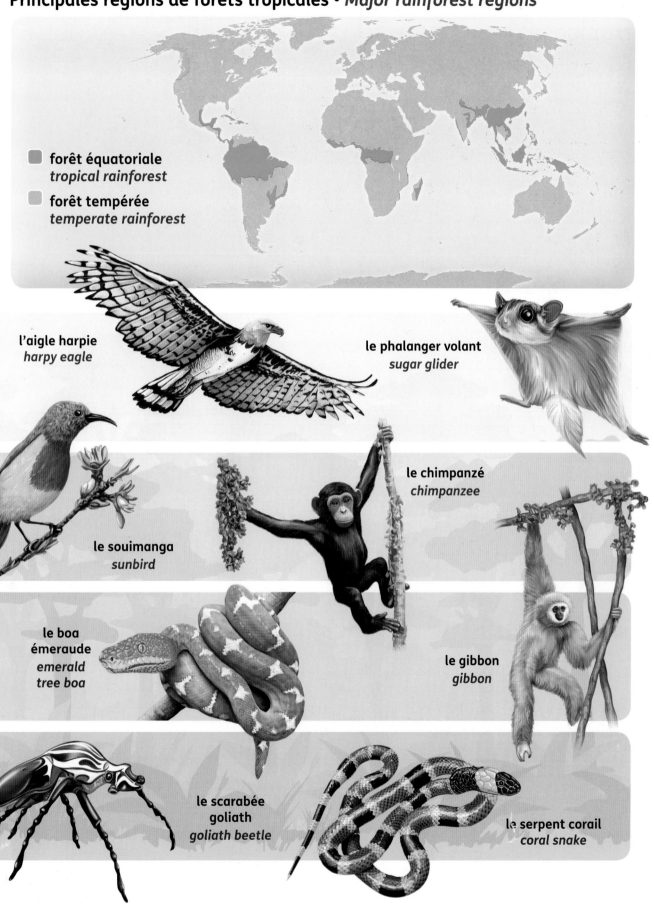

forêt équatoriale
tropical rainforest

forêt tempérée
temperate rainforest

l'aigle harpie
harpy eagle

le phalanger volant
sugar glider

le souimanga
sunbird

le chimpanzé
chimpanzee

**le boa
émeraude**
*emerald
tree boa*

le gibbon
gibbon

**le scarabée
goliath**
goliath beetle

le serpent corail
coral snake

La vie sur le sol des forêts tropicales humides *(vertical, left margin)*

La vie sur le sol des forêts tropicales humides
Life on the rainforest floor

Très peu de lumière atteint le sol forestier. Les insectes et les reptiles vivent parmi les feuilles et les enchevêtrements de lianes, tandis que les mammifères et les oiseaux qui ne volent pas se frayent un chemin à travers les troncs d'arbres.

Very little light reaches the forest floor. Insects and reptiles live among leaves and tangled vines, while mammals and flightless birds weave their way through the tree trunks.

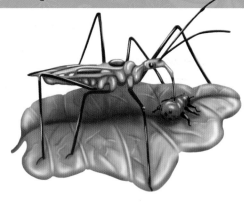

la punaise assassine • *assassin bug*
Les punaises assassines injectent une salive mortelle dans leurs proies qui liquéfie leurs organes internes.
Assassin bugs inject their prey with a deadly saliva that turns body contents to liquid.

le jaguar • *jaguar*
Les jaguars rôdent dans les broussailles et grimpent aussi dans le sous-bois.
Jaguars prowl through the undergrowth and also climb up into the understorey.

le tapir
tapir

le dynaste hercules
Hercules beetle

l'araignée mygale
funnel web spider

le bupreste
jewel beetle

les fourmis soldats
army ants

Rainforest creatures

le serpent de vigne
vine snake

le gorille des plaines
lowland gorilla

l'okapi
okapi

l'éléphant de forêt d'Afrique
African forest elephant

le kiwi • *kiwi*
Le kiwi vit dans les forêts
tempérées humides de
Nouvelle-Zélande.
*Kiwis live in the temperate
rainforests of New Zealand.*

**la fourmi
coupe-feuille**
leafcutter ant

le casoar
cassowary

l'araignée goliath • *goliath spider*
L'araignée goliath est assez grande
pour s'attaquer à de petits oiseaux.
*The goliath spider is large enough to
prey on small birds.*

Les animaux de la canopée • *Creatures of the canopy*

Il y a plus d'animaux dans la canopée que dans n'importe quelle autre couche de la forêt tropicale.

The canopy is home to more creatures than any other layer of the rainforest.

le lémur
lemur

le loriquet à tête bleue
rainbow lorikeet

l'orang-outan
orang-utan

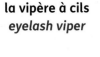

le méliphage
honeyeater

la vipère à cils
eyelash viper

le singe capucin
capuchin monkey

la mante religieuse géante des forêts tropicales
giant rainforest praying mantis
La mante religieuse a ce nom car on dirait qu'elle prie.
The praying mantis was given its name because it looks as though it is praying.

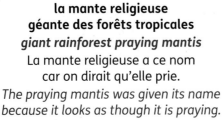

le kangourou arboricole
tree kangaroo

Rainforest creatures

le colibri
hummingbird

Le colibri étend sa longue langue pour aspirer le nectar des fleurs.
The hummingbird extends its long tongue to suck nectar from flowers.

le colugo
colugo

l'escargot des arbres
tree snail

le gecko volant
flying gecko

le singe colobe
colobus monkey

le tarsier
tarsier

le scarabée girafe
giraffe weevil

Le scarabée girafe utilise son très long cou pour se défendre.
The giraffe weevil uses its very long neck to help it fight.

Des couleurs pour prévenir
Warning colours

Certains animaux arborent des couleurs très vives pour prévenir les prédateurs de leur toxicité.

Some creatures are very brightly coloured to warn predators that they are poisonous.

les dendrobates • *poison dart frogs*

Les dendrobates ont la peau toxique. Les Indiens d'Amazonie utilisent ce poison sur le bout de leurs flèches.
Poison dart frogs were given their name because the rainforest people dipped their hunting darts in the frogs' poison.

Dans la forêt tropicale amazonienne

In the Amazon rainforest

La forêt tropicale amazonienne abrite des millions d'espèces d'animaux. Ceux représentés ici vivent dans la canopée amazonienne.

The Amazon rainforest contains millions of animal species. The creatures shown here live in the Amazon canopy.

1 l'ara rouge
scarlet macaw

2 le singe laineux
woolly monkey

3 le perroquet amazone
Amazon parrot

4 le papillon morpho
morpho butterfly

5 l'iguane vert
green iguana

6 le paresseux à trois doigts
three-toed sloth

7 le singe-araignée
spider monkey

8 le coati
coatimundi

9 le toucan à carène
keel-billed toucan

10 le ouistiti pygmée
pygmy marmoset

11 le singe hurleur
howler monkey

12 le dendrobate
poison dart frog

Les forêts sont l'habitat d'un nombre incalculable de créatures, grandes ou petites...

Forests are home to countless creatures, large and small...

LA FAUNE DES FORÊTS ET DES TERRES BOISÉES
FOREST AND WOODLAND WILDLIFE

Les habitats des forêts • *Forest habitats*

Il existe deux grandes catégories de forêts dans les parties les plus froides du monde : les forêts à feuilles caduques, c'est-à-dire les forêts avec des arbres qui perdent leurs feuilles en hiver ; et les forêts sempervirentes, qui ont des arbres qui restent verts toute l'année.

There are two main types of forest in the cooler parts of the world. Deciduous forests have trees that shed their leaves in winter. Evergreen forests have trees that stay green all year round.

Les forêts à feuilles caduques et les terres boisées
Deciduous forests and woodlands

On trouve les forêts à feuilles caduques surtout dans les régions où il pleut beaucoup.

Deciduous forests grow in regions where there is plenty of rain.

le citron
brimstone butterfly

l'escargot des jardins
garden snail

le pic épeiche
woodpecker

le daim
fallow deer

le tamia
chipmunk

Principales régions de forêts à feuilles caduques et sempervirentes
Major regions of deciduous and evergreen forest

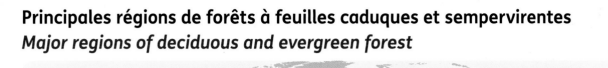

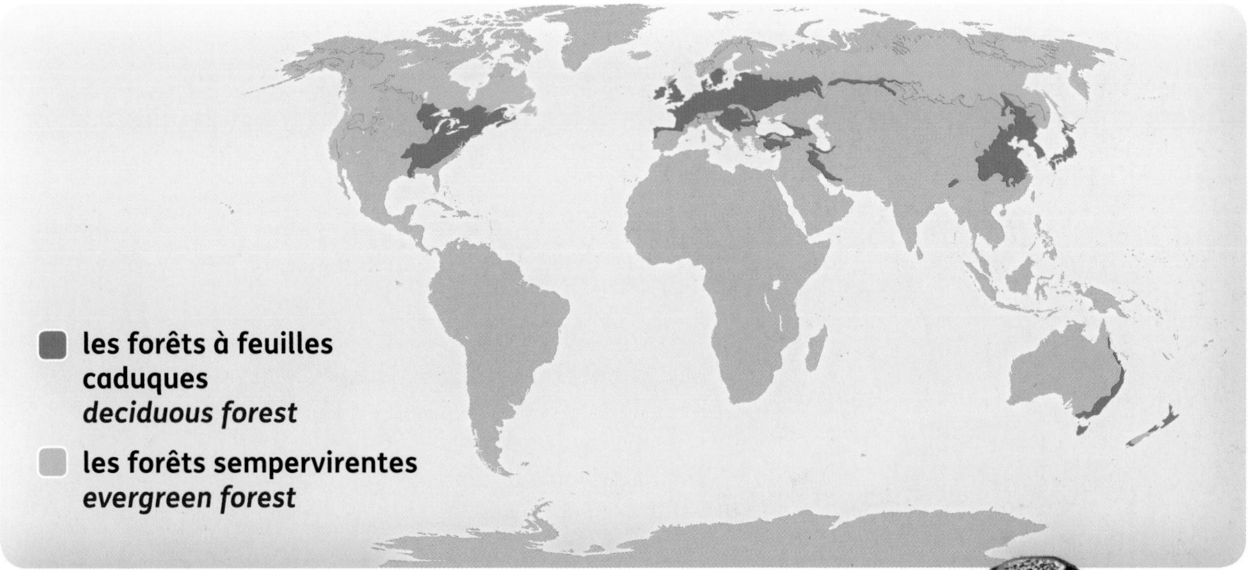

■ les forêts à feuilles
caduques
deciduous forest

□ les forêts sempervirentes
evergreen forest

Les forêts sempervirentes • *Evergreen forests*

On les trouve surtout dans les régions aux hivers longs et enneigés et aux étés courts et tempérés.

Evergreen forests mostly grow in places with long, snowy winters and short, cool summers.

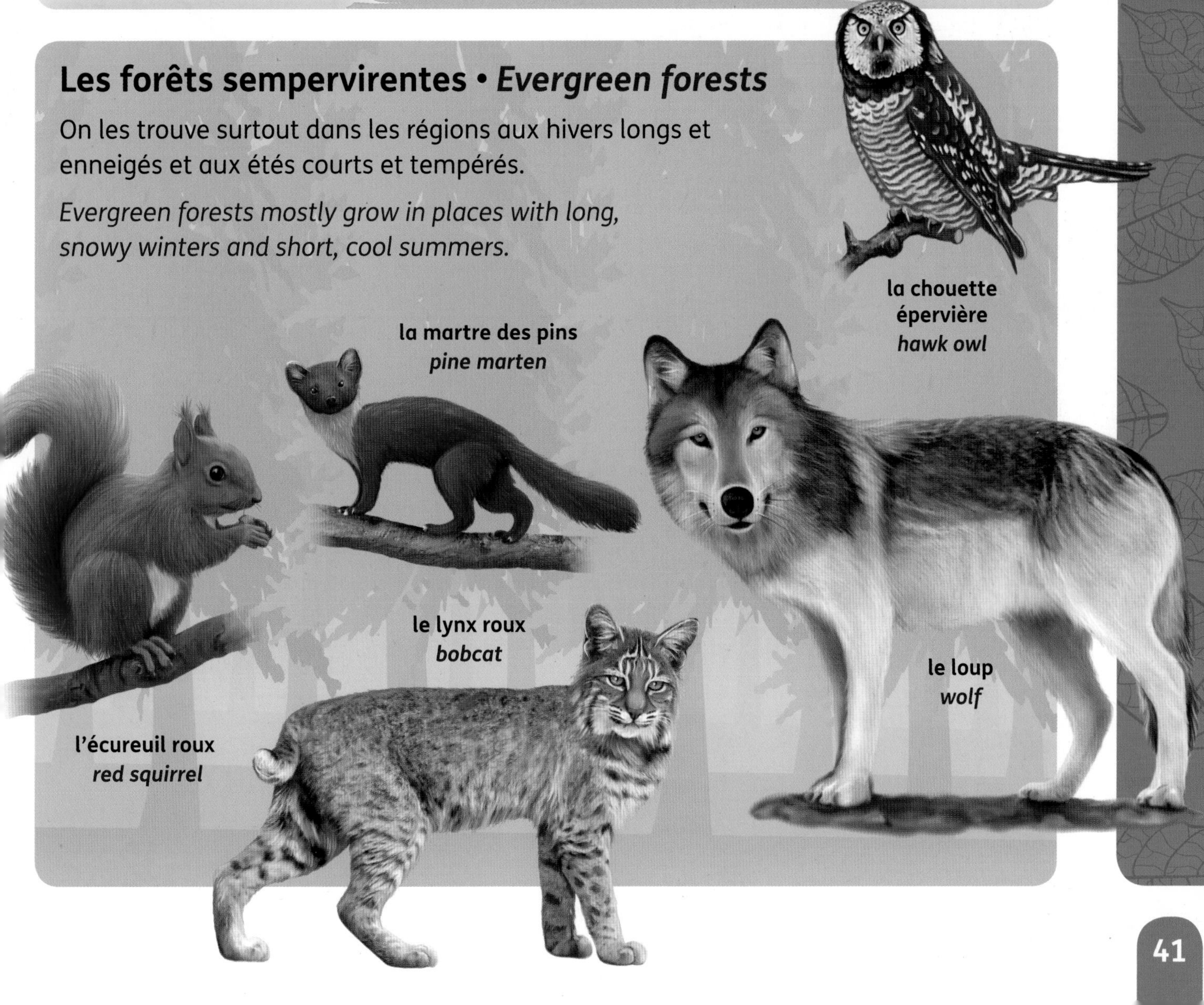

la chouette
épervière
hawk owl

la martre des pins
pine marten

le lynx roux
bobcat

le loup
wolf

l'écureuil roux
red squirrel

Les animaux de la forêt à feuilles caduques
Deciduous forest creatures

Beaucoup des animaux des forêts à feuilles caduques se nourrissent de fruits à coque, de baies et d'insectes. Quand les arbres perdent leurs feuilles, la plupart de mammifères hibernent.

Many animals in deciduous forests feed on nuts, berries and insects. When the trees lose their leaves, most mammals hibernate.

le rossignol • *nightingale*
Le rossignol est connu pour son chant ravissant.
The nightingale is famous for its beautiful song.

le dindon sauvage • *wild turkey*
Les dindons sauvages vivent en toute liberté dans certaines forêts d'Amérique du Nord.
Wild turkeys roam free in some American woodlands.

le cerf élaphe
red deer
Certains animaux, comme le cerf élaphe et l'écureuil gris, vivent aussi bien dans les forêts à feuilles caduques que dans les forêts de sempervirent.
Some creatures, like red deer and grey squirrels, live in both deciduous and evergreen forests.

le raton laveur
raccoon

42

Forest and woodland wildlife

la belette
weasel

le pouillot siffleur
wood warbler

le pigeon ramier
wood pigeon

l'écureuil gris
grey squirrel

le diable de Tasmanie • *Tasmanian devil*
Le diable de Tasmanie se trouve uniquement en Tasmanie, en Australie.
The Tasmanian devil is only found in Tasmania, Australia.

le renard roux
red fox

la hulotte • *tawny owl*
La hulotte est aussi connue sous le nom de chat-huant.
The tawny owl is also known as the brown owl.

Sur le sol de la forêt
Life on a woodland floor

Cette scène présente des animaux dans une forêt de feuillus. Certains creusent des terriers, d'autres vivent dans le terreau de feuilles qui recouvre le sol de la forêt.

This scene shows creatures in a deciduous woodland. Some dig burrows in the earth. Some live in the leaf mould on the forest floor.

1 l'hermine
stoat

2 la taupe
mole

3 le blaireau
badger

4 le loir
dormouse

5 la musaraigne
shrew

6 le hérisson • *hedgehog*
Les hérissons se protègent avec leurs piquants.
Hedgehogs are protected by spiny quills.

Les animaux du terreau
Creatures in the leaf mould

7 le cloporte
woodlouse

8 le mille-pattes
centipede

9 le ver de terre
earthworm

10 le mille-pattes
millipede

La faune des forêts sempervirentes
Evergreen forest wildlife

Les animaux des forêts sempervirentes doivent résister aux hivers glacials et enneigés. Certains mammifères se munissent de fourrures épaisses, d'autres hibernent. Les oiseaux migrent généralement vers le sud pour l'hiver.

Creatures in an evergreen forest need to cope with freezing, snowy winters. Some mammals grow thick coats and some hibernate. Birds usually migrate south for the winter.

le geai de Steller
Steller's jay

l'ours noir
black bear

la mouffette • skunk
Lorsqu'elle se croit attaquée, la mouffette lance un jet de liquide nauséabond.
If they are attacked, skunks release a very strong smelling spray.

le lynx
lynx

Forest and woodland wildlife

le grimpereau
treecreeper

la chouette lapone
great grey owl
Les chouettes
sont des animaux
nocturnes.
Elles chassent donc
généralement la nuit.
*Owls are nocturnal,
so they usually hunt
at night.*

le putois
polecat

l'élan • moose
L'élan mâle utilise ses
énormes bois pour se battre
contre d'autres mâles.
*The male moose uses
its giant antlers
to fight other males.*

le carcajou, le glouton
wolverine

le porc-épic
porcupine

47

Les aigles volent parmi les hauts sommets...

Eagles soar among the high mountain peaks...

LES ANIMAUX DE LA MONTAGNE
MOUNTAIN ANIMALS

Les animaux de la montagne

Les habitats des montagnes • *Mountain habitats*

Des montagnes se trouvent dans tous les continents du monde. Les Andes, les Rocheuses, l'Himalaya et les Alpes sont toutes de grandes chaînes de montagnes.

Mountains are found in all the world's continents. The Andes, the Rockies, the Himalayas and the Alps are all major mountain ranges.

Les étages supérieurs et inférieurs des montagnes
Upper and lower slopes

La plupart des montagnes offrent deux habitats différents : les pentes supérieures raides (l'étage nival) sont nues, rocailleuses et souvent recouvertes de neige. Les pentes inférieures, plus douces (l'étage alpin), sont généralement recouvertes d'arbres.

Most mountains provide two different habitats. The steep upper slopes are bare and rocky and often blanketed with snow. The gentle lower slopes are generally covered with trees.

Les étages supérieurs
Upper slopes

la chèvre de montagne
mountain goat

le gypaète barbu
bearded vulture

Les étages inférieurs
Lower slopes

la vigogne
vicuña

le panda roux
red panda

Mountain animals

Les grandes chaînes de montagnes • *Major mountain ranges*

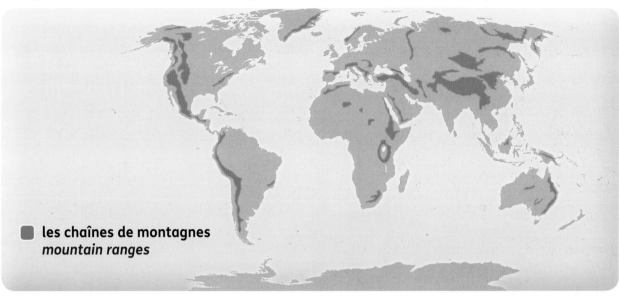

les chaînes de montagnes
mountain ranges

le léopard des neiges
snow leopard

le chinchilla
chinchilla

la perruche de Pennant
crimson rosella

le gorille de
montagne
mountain gorilla

La vie dans les montagnes • *Life in the mountains*

Trouver de quoi se nourrir et de quoi s'abriter sur les sommets des montagnes est difficile. C'est pourquoi les animaux comme le chamois et le couguar se déplacent entre les différents étages de la montagne. La plupart des autres animaux restent dans les forêts des montagnes.

Finding food and shelter on the mountain tops is hard, so animals like the chamois and cougar move between the upper and lower slopes. Most other creatures stay in the highland forests.

le chamois
chamois

le couguar • *cougar*
Le puma est un autre nom pour le couguar.
Puma is another name for cougar.

le milan royal
red kite

la buse variable
common buzzard

Les oiseaux de montagne
Mountain birds

Un grand nombre d'oiseaux de proie chassent sur les pentes des montagnes où ils peuvent facilement repérer leurs proies. Mais ils sont à l'aise dans d'autres habitats aussi, tels que les plaines.

Many birds of prey hunt on mountain slopes where they can easily spot their prey. But they are also at home in other habitats, such as grasslands.

le faucon pèlerin
peregrine falcon

l'aigle royal
golden eagle

Mountain animals

Les animaux domestiqués • *Domesticated creatures*

Certains animaux de montagne ont été domestiqués par l'homme. Ils ont été sélectionnés pour l'élevage comme animaux de travail, animaux de compagnie ou pour la ferme.

Some mountain creatures have been domesticated by humans. They have been bred as working animals, pets and farm animals.

le lama
llama

le yak
yak

l'alpaga
alpaca

le cobaye • *cavy*
Les cobayes sont les ancêtres sauvages des cochons d'Inde.
Cavies are the wild ancestors of guinea pigs.

le panda géant
giant panda
Les pandas géants sont en voie de disparition.
Giant pandas are in danger of becoming extinct.

le bouquetin
ibex

Dans les vastes prairies, les chasseurs guettent leur proie...

On the wide open grasslands, hunters lie in wait for their prey...

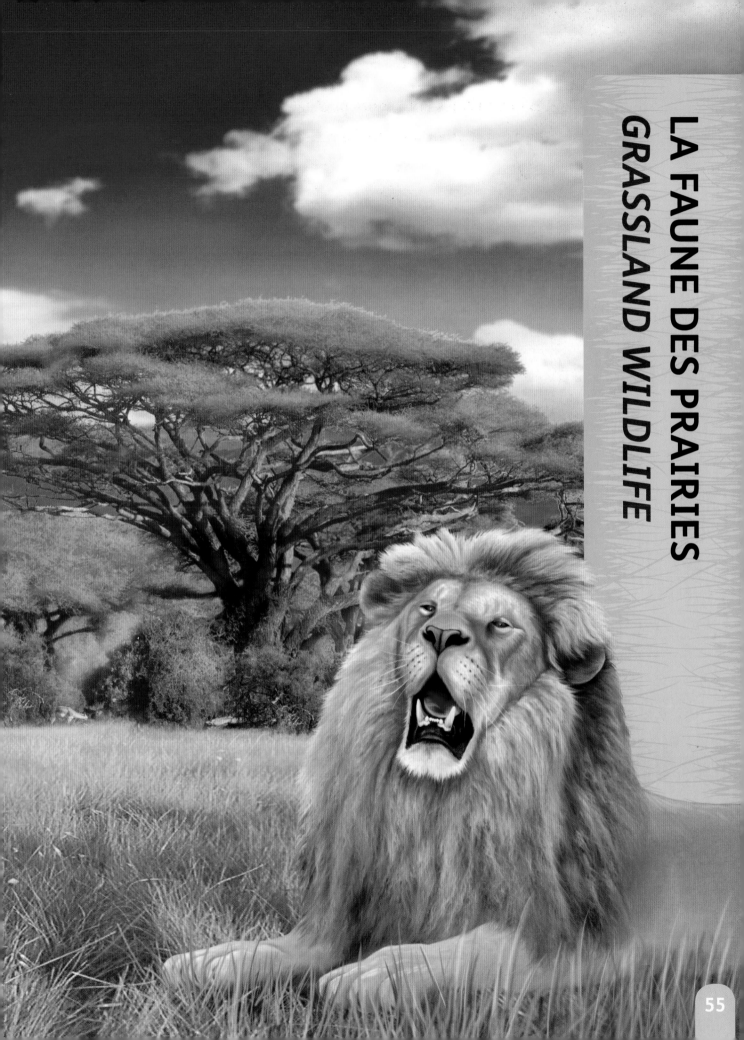

LA FAUNE DES PRAIRIES
GRASSLAND WILDLIFE

Les habitats des prairies • *Grassland habitats*

Les plaines sont de vastes étendues d'herbes et d'arbustes sauvages. On les trouve aussi bien dans les régions froides que chaudes.

Grasslands are large stretches of ground covered with wild grasses and shrubs. They are found in both hot and cold regions.

Les prairies chaudes et sèches
Hot, dry grasslands

Les plaines à saisons sèches, propres aux régions chaudes, s'appellent savanes. On les trouve en Afrique, en Asie et en Amérique du Sud.

Some hot, dry grasslands are called savannahs. There are savannahs in Africa, Asia and South America.

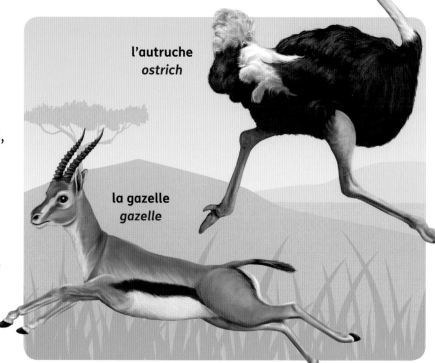

l'autruche
ostrich

la gazelle
gazelle

Les prairies tempérées
Cooler grasslands

Les plaines d'Amérique du Nord s'appellent les Grandes Prairies. L'été y est chaud et l'hiver froid et humide.

The grasslands of North America are called the Prairies. They have hot summers and cold, wet winters.

le bison
bison

le lièvre des prairies
jackrabbit

Grassland wildlife

Les principales zones des grandes plaines • *Major grassland regions*

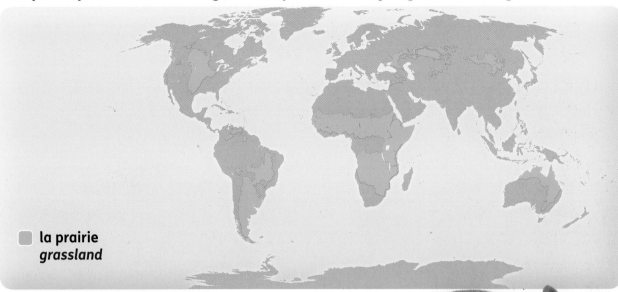

◻ la prairie
grassland

La brousse et la broussaille
Bush and scrub

De nombreuses régions de l'Australie sont couvertes d'herbes et de broussailles. Ces régions chaudes et sèches sont connues sous le nom de bush australien.

Many parts of Australia are covered with grass and scrub. These hot, dry regions are known as the bush.

le wombat
wombat

le goanna
goanna

la vipère
common adder

le faisan
pheasant

Les landes
Moorlands

Les landes se trouvent dans les régions froides et pluvieuses. Elles sont composées de petits buissons et arbustes qui fournissent d'excellents abris pour la faune.

Moors are found in cool regions with plenty of rain. They have low bushes and shrubs which provide good cover for wildlife.

Dans la savane • *On the savannah*

La savane africaine abrite de nombreux animaux vivant en troupeau. Ils parcourent de longues distances à la recherche d'eau et sont souvent la proie de chasseurs.

On the African savannah, many animals live in herds. They travel large distances in search of water, and they are often in danger from hunters.

❶
le lion
lion

❷
le buffle
buffalo

❸
le zèbre
zebra

Grassland wildlife

4
la girafe
giraffe

5
le guépard
cheetah

6
l'éléphant africain
African elephant

7
l'antilope
antelope

D'autres animaux de la savane
More savannah creatures

De nombreux animaux de la savane échappent à leurs prédateurs en courant très vite. D'autres creusent des terriers pour rester en sécurité.

Many animals on the savannah escape from predators by running very fast. Some burrow underground to stay safe.

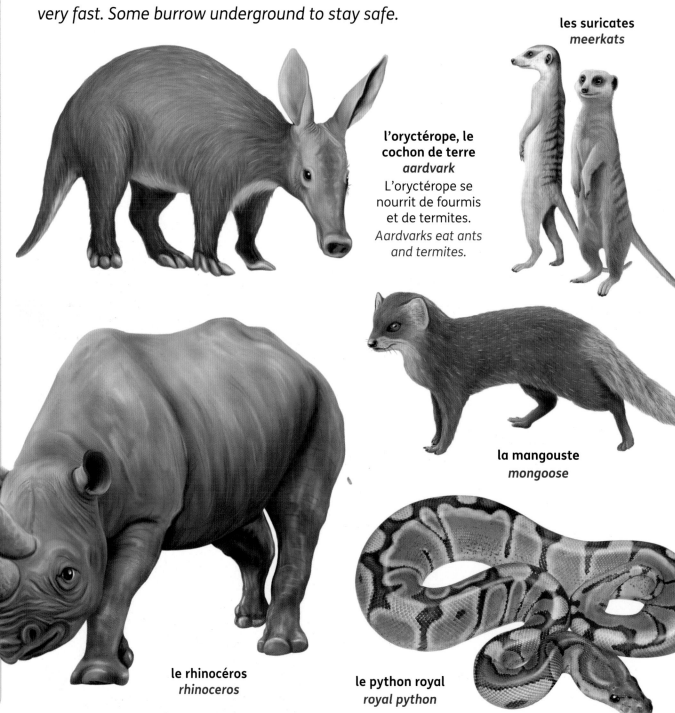

les suricates
meerkats

l'oryctérope, le cochon de terre
aardvark
L'oryctérope se nourrit de fourmis et de termites.
Aardvarks eat ants and termites.

la mangouste
mongoose

le rhinocéros
rhinoceros

le python royal
royal python

Grassland wildlife

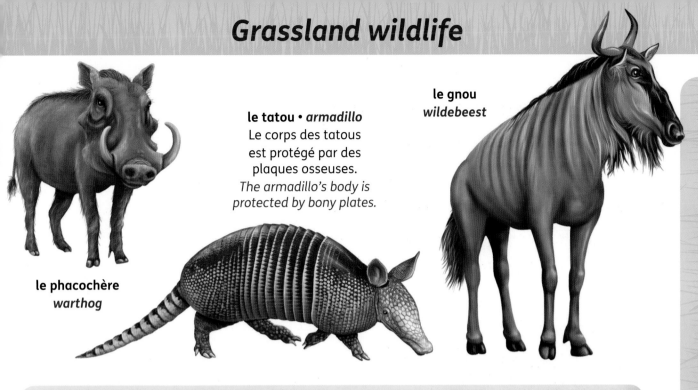

le tatou • *armadillo*
Le corps des tatous est protégé par des plaques osseuses.
The armadillo's body is protected by bony plates.

le gnou
wildebeest

le phacochère
warthog

La termitière • *Termite mound*

Les termites vivent en colonie avec une seule reine, beaucoup plus grosse que ses sujets. Ils construisent un monticule de terre pour elle afin qu'elle puisse pondre ses œufs et donner ainsi naissance à tous les jeunes de la termitière.

Termites live in colonies with a single large queen. They build a mound to house their queen, and she lays eggs which will hatch to form all the young in the colony.

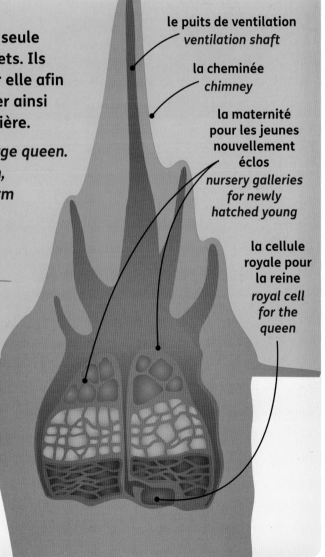

le puits de ventilation
ventilation shaft

la cheminée
chimney

la maternité pour les jeunes nouvellement éclos
nursery galleries for newly hatched young

la cellule royale pour la reine
royal cell for the queen

le termite • *termite*
Les termites sont parfois appelées fourmis blanches.
Termites are sometimes called white ants.

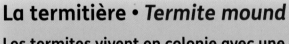

la termitière en coupe transversale
cutaway termite mound

Les termites ouvrières construisent de grands monticules de terre et de salive.

Termite workers build mounds from earth and saliva.

La faune des plaines et des landes
Grassland and moorland wildlife

Les animaux des plaines et des landes sont généralement très bien camouflés. Certains oiseaux des landes, comme les lagopèdes et les perdrix, volent près du sol en utilisant les buissons comme couverture.

Grassland and moorland animals are usually very well camouflaged. Some moorland birds, such as grouse and partridges, fly close to the ground using bushes as cover.

le petit paon de nuit
emperor moth

la pintade
guinea fowl

le coyote • *coyote*
Le coyote vit dans la Grande Prairie d'Amérique du Nord.
Coyotes live on the North American prairies.

le lagopède d'Écosse
red grouse

Grassland wildlife

l'alouette
skylark

la crécerelle
kestrel

le lièvre
hare

la sauterelle
grasshopper

la perdrix
partridge

le chien de prairie
prairie dog
Le chien de prairie
est une sorte
d'écureuil terrestre.
*The prairie dog is
a kind of ground
squirrel.*

le furet
ferret

Dans le bush australien *Dans le bush australien*

Dans le bush australien • *In the bush*

Le bush australien comprend des touffes d'herbes dures, des arbustes rabougris et des eucalyptus dispersés. Cette brousse est le lieu d'habitation d'un grand nombre d'animaux que l'on ne trouve nulle part ailleurs.

In the Australian bush, there are rough grasses, scrubby bushes and scattered eucalyptus trees. The bush is home to many creatures that are not found anywhere else in the world.

1
le kangourou • *red kangaroo*

2
le dingo • *dingo*

3
le scinque à langue bleue
blue-tongued skink

4
l'échidné australien
spiny anteater

5
le wallaby • *wallaby*
Les wallabies ressemblent à de petits kangourous.
Wallabies look like small kangaroos.

6
le cacatoès rosalbin
galah

7
le bilby,
le bandicoot
lapin
bilby

8
l'émeu • *emu*
Les émeus ne peuvent pas
voler, mais ils courent très vite.
*Emus cannot fly but they
can run very fast.*

9
le cacatoès • *cockatoo*

11
la perruche
budgerigar

10
le bandicoot • *bandicoot*

12
le koala
koala

Les alligators se tapissent dans les marais ombragés...

Alligators lurk in shady swamps...

LA FAUNE DES RIVIÈRES, DES LACS ET DES ZONES HUMIDES
RIVER, LAKE AND WETLAND WILDLIFE

Les habitats près de l'eau

Les habitats près de l'eau • *Water habitats*

Les rivières, les lacs, les étangs et les zones humides offrent une grande variété d'habitats pour la faune vivant dans l'eau. Ils fournissent aussi un habitat pour les animaux terrestres qui vivent au bord de l'eau.

Rivers, lakes, ponds and wetlands provide a range of habitats for water-dwelling creatures. They are also home to land-dwelling animals that live on the water's edge.

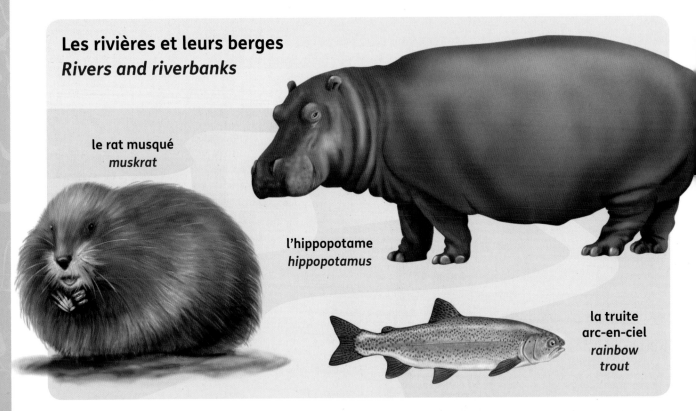

Les rivières et leurs berges
Rivers and riverbanks

le rat musqué
muskrat

l'hippopotame
hippopotamus

la truite
arc-en-ciel
*rainbow
trout*

Les lacs et les étangs
Lakes and ponds

l'agrion
damselfly

le poisson-chat
catfish

la foulque
coot

River, lake and wetland wildlife

Les fleuves • *Major rivers*

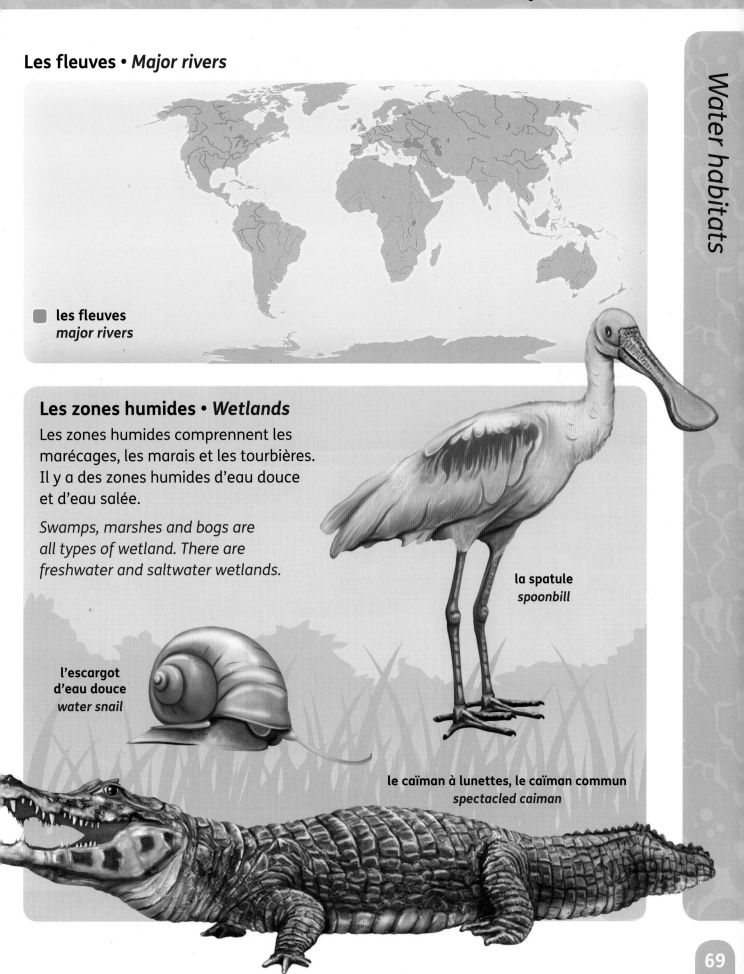

■ **les fleuves**
major rivers

Les zones humides • *Wetlands*

Les zones humides comprennent les marécages, les marais et les tourbières. Il y a des zones humides d'eau douce et d'eau salée.

Swamps, marshes and bogs are all types of wetland. There are freshwater and saltwater wetlands.

la spatule
spoonbill

l'escargot d'eau douce
water snail

le caïman à lunettes, le caïman commun
spectacled caiman

La faune des rivières • *River creatures*

L'eau des rivières peut être relativement chaude ou glaciale, peu profonde ou très profonde. Le courant peut être rapide ou lent. Chaque type de rivière est le milieu de vie de toute une variété d'animaux.

Rivers can be warm or icy, shallow or deep, fast- or slow-moving.
Each type of river is home to a different range of wildlife.

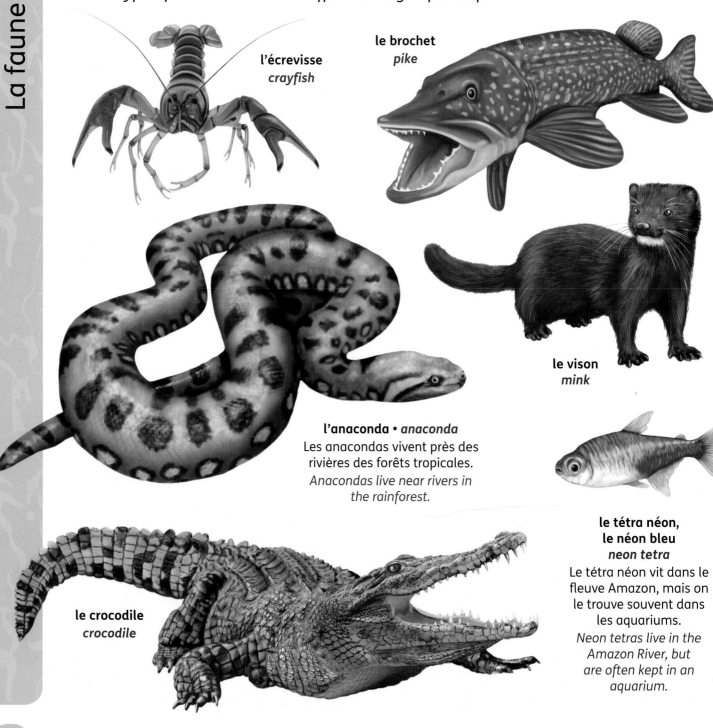

l'écrevisse
crayfish

le brochet
pike

le vison
mink

l'anaconda • *anaconda*
Les anacondas vivent près des rivières des forêts tropicales.
Anacondas live near rivers in the rainforest.

le tétra néon,
le néon bleu
neon tetra
Le tétra néon vit dans le fleuve Amazon, mais on le trouve souvent dans les aquariums.
Neon tetras live in the Amazon River, but are often kept in an aquarium.

le crocodile
crocodile

70

River, lake and wetland wildlife

le ragondin
coypu

l'anguille électrique • *electric eel*
L'anguille électrique assomme sa proie avec une décharge électrique.
The electric eel stuns its prey with an electric shock.

le piranha • *piranha*
Les piranhas utilisent leurs dents acérées pour déchiqueter la chair de leurs proies.
Piranhas use their very sharp teeth to strip the flesh off other creatures.

le platypus • *platypus*
Le platypus est un mammifère qui pond des œufs. On ne le trouve qu'en Australie.
The platypus is a mammal that lays eggs. It is only found in Australia.

La hutte du castor • *Beaver lodge*

Les castors utilisent des branches pour construire leurs abris appelés huttes.
Beavers use twigs to build a home called a lodge.

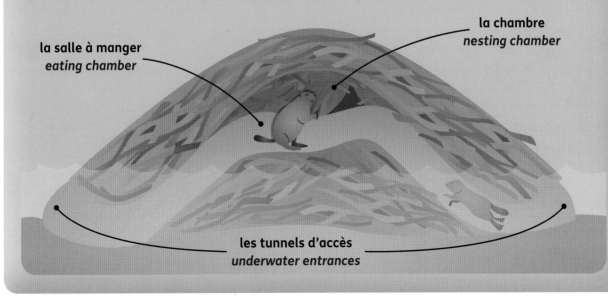

la chambre
nesting chamber

la salle à manger
eating chamber

les tunnels d'accès
underwater entrances

71

La vie sur la rivière
Life on the river

Les rivières servent d'habitat à quantité d'animaux. Les mammifères vivent dans des terriers creusés dans la berge. Les canards et les cygnes glissent sur l'eau, et d'autres oiseaux attrapent des poissons et des insectes.

Rivers provide a habitat for many creatures. Mammals live in burrows in the river bank. Ducks and swans glide over the water's surface, and birds catch fish and insects.

1 le héron
heron

2 le cincle
dipper

3 le rat taupier
water vole

4 la musaraigne d'eau
water shrew

5 la poule d'eau
moorhen

6 le cygne
swan

7 le martin-pêcheur
kingfisher

8 la loutre
otter

9 le colvert
mallard

10 la grenouille
common frog

Les insectes et les petites bestioles
Insects and minibeasts

11 l'araignée d'eau
pondskater

12 la libellule
dragonfly

13 la notonecte glauque
greater water boatman

14 l'éphémère
mayfly

La faune des lacs et des étangs • *Lake and pond wildlife*

La plupart des lacs et des étangs ont des eaux douces,
bien qu'il existe quelques lacs d'eau salée.

*Most lakes and ponds are freshwater environments,
although there are a few saltwater lakes.*

**la tortue
serpentine**
*snapping
turtle*

la grenouille-taureau
American bullfrog

le pélican
pelican

le crapaud commun • *common toad*
On trouve souvent les crapauds à
proximité des étangs.
Toads are often found close to ponds.

le flamant
flamingo

le capybara
capybara

River, lake and wetland wildlife

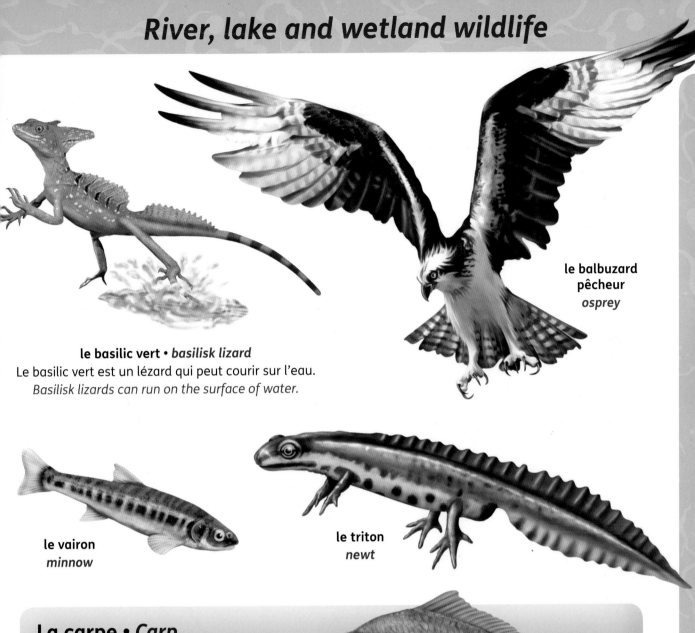

le balbuzard pêcheur
osprey

le basilic vert • *basilisk lizard*
Le basilic vert est un lézard qui peut courir sur l'eau.
Basilisk lizards can run on the surface of water.

le vairon
minnow

le triton
newt

La carpe • *Carp*

La carpe vit dans les lacs. Les poissons rouges et les carpes koï sont des carpes d'élevage.

The common carp is found in lakes. Goldfish and koi are domesticated species of carp.

la carpe
common carp

le poisson rouge
goldfish

la carpe koï
koi

75

Les animaux des zones humides • *Wetland animals*

Les régions souvent inondées et gorgées d'eau s'appellent des zones humides. Elles comprennent les marécages, les tourbières, les marais, les roselières, ainsi que les terres autour des estuaires.

Regions that are often flooded and waterlogged are known as wetlands. They include swamps, bogs, marshes, fens, reed beds and the land around river estuaries.

l'ibis
ibis

la grue
crane

le dipneuste • *lungfish*
Le dipneuste est un poisson qui, en plus de branchies, possède des poumons qui lui permettent de respirer en dehors de l'eau en saison sèche.
Lungfish have lungs as well as gills so they can breathe air during a dry season.

l'alligator
alligator

River, lake and wetland wildlife

**la tortue à
dos diamanté**
diamondback terrapin

la cigogne
stork

Les grands félins du marais
Big cats of the swamp

Certains grands félins vivent
dans les mangroves, mais ils
sont menacés d'extinction.

*Some big cats live in mangrove
swamps, but they are in danger
of becoming extinct.*

**la panthère
de Floride**
*Florida
panther*

**le tigre du
Bengale**
Bengal tiger

Dans le désert, les dunes s'étendent sur des kilomètres sous un soleil de plomb...

In the desert, sand dunes stretch for miles under a baking sun...

LA FAUNE DU DÉSERT
DESERT WILDLIFE

Les habitats du désert • *Desert habitats*

Les déserts sont de vastes régions de terres arides avec de rares précipitations. Certains sont chauds et sablonneux, d'autres froids et rocailleux.

Deserts are vast regions of arid land with almost no rainfall. Some are hot and sandy. Others are cold and rocky.

Les déserts chauds • *Hot deserts*

Les déserts chauds ont des températures très élevées pendant le jour et basses pendant la nuit. De puissants vents balayent les dunes et soulèvent les tempêtes de sable.

Hot deserts have scorching days and cold nights. Powerful winds race across the dunes and whip up sandstorms.

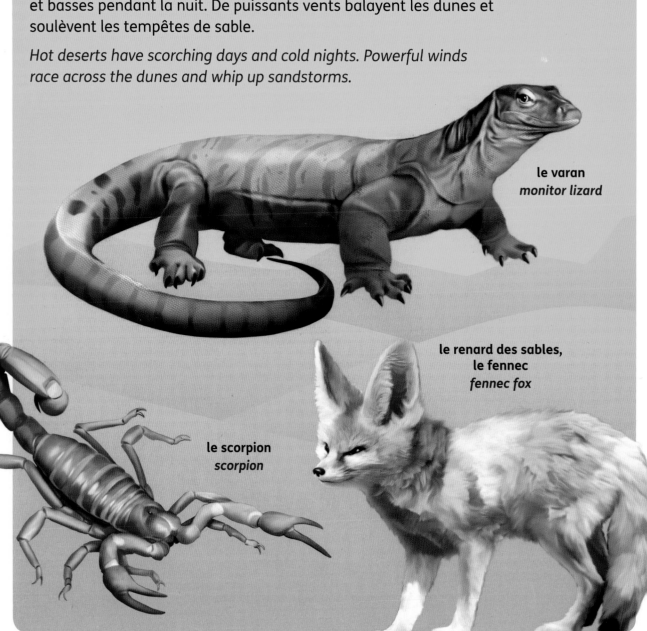

le varan
monitor lizard

**le renard des sables,
le fennec**
fennec fox

le scorpion
scorpion

Carte des principaux déserts du monde
Map of the world's main desert regions

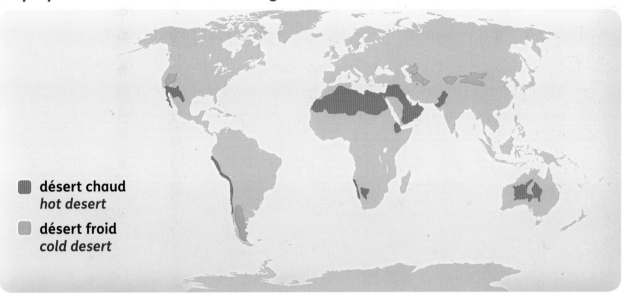

- ■ **désert chaud**
  hot desert
- ■ **désert froid**
  cold desert

Les déserts froids • *Cold deserts*

Il peut faire chaud pendant la journée dans les déserts froids, mais les températures tombent bien en-dessous de zéro pendant la nuit.

Cold deserts can be warm during the day, but temperatures at night drop well below freezing point.

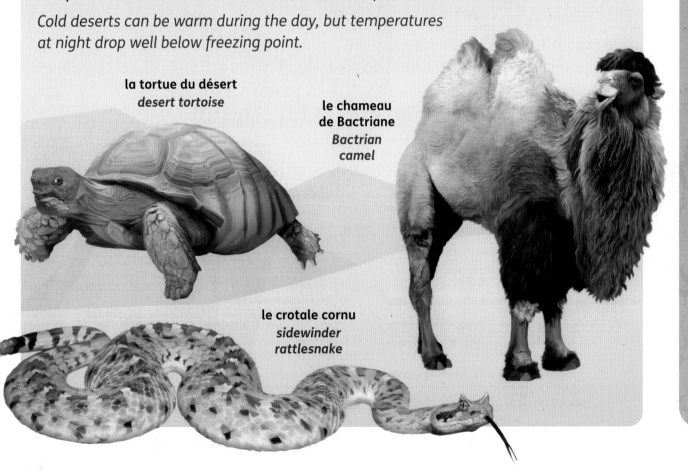

la tortue du désert
desert tortoise

le chameau de Bactriane
Bactrian camel

le crotale cornu
sidewinder rattlesnake

Les animaux du désert • *Desert creatures*

Les animaux du désert doivent survivre dans un environnement très dur et avec très peu d'eau. Certains peuvent stocker du liquide dans leur corps, d'autres se terrent sous le sable pour rester au frais.

Desert animals have to survive in a very harsh environment with almost no water. Some are able to store liquid in their bodies. Some burrow under the sand to keep cool.

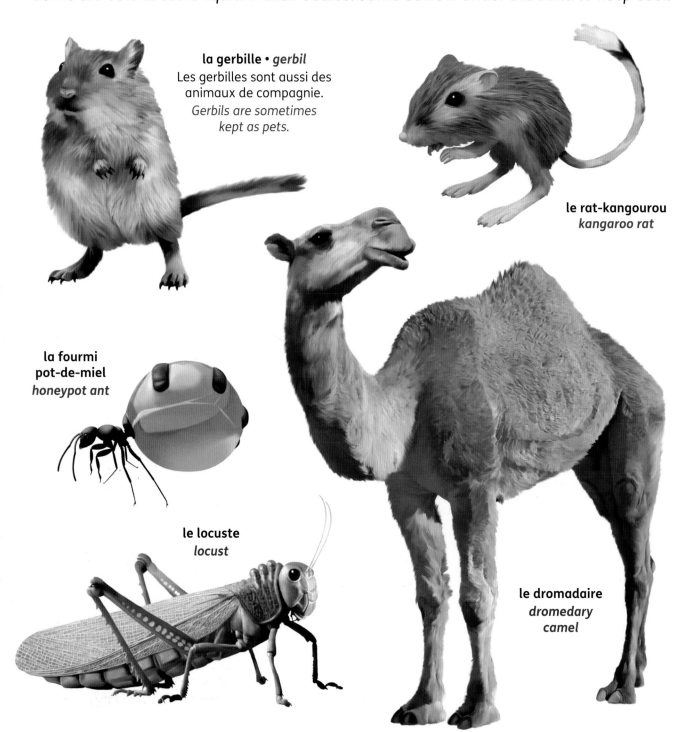

la gerbille • *gerbil*
Les gerbilles sont aussi des animaux de compagnie.
Gerbils are sometimes kept as pets.

le rat-kangourou
kangaroo rat

la fourmi pot-de-miel
honeypot ant

le locuste
locust

le dromadaire
dromedary camel

Desert wildlife

l'urubu à tête rouge
turkey vulture
Les urubus, comme les autres vautours, se nourrissent de la chair d'animaux morts, que l'on appelle charognes.
Vultures feed on the flesh of dead animals, known as carrion.

la veuve noire
black widow spider

la vipère à cornes
horned desert viper

la gerboise • *jerboa*
Les grandes oreilles de la gerboise lui permettent de baisser la température de son corps.
The enormous ears of the jerboa allow it to lose body heat rapidly.

le géocoucou
roadrunner

le taïpan du désert • *inland taipan*
Le taïpan du désert est un des serpents les plus venimeux du monde.
The inland taipan is one of the world's most venomous snakes.

Les raies manta glissent silencieusement dans l'océan...

Manta rays glide silently through the ocean...

LA VIE DANS L'OCÉAN
LIFE IN THE OCEAN

La vie dans l'océan

Les océans • *Oceans*

Plus des deux-tiers de la surface de la Terre est recouverte d'eau.
Il existe cinq océans et de nombreuses mers.

More than two-thirds of the Earth's surface is covered by water.
There are five oceans and several seas.

Les zones océaniques • *Ocean zones*

Les océans comportent différentes zones. Chaque zone possède sa propre faune, mais certains animaux se déplacent entre les zones.

Oceans have different zones. Each zone has its own wildlife, although some creatures move between zones.

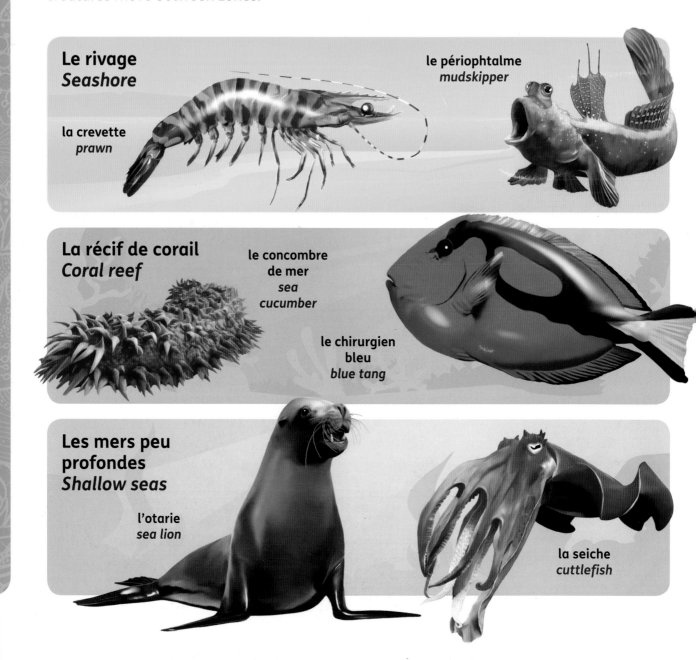

Le rivage
Seashore

la crevette
prawn

le périophtalme
mudskipper

La récif de corail
Coral reef

le concombre
de mer
sea
cucumber

le chirurgien
bleu
blue tang

Les mers peu profondes
Shallow seas

l'otarie
sea lion

la seiche
cuttlefish

Life in the ocean

Carte des mers et océans principaux • *Map of major oceans and seas*

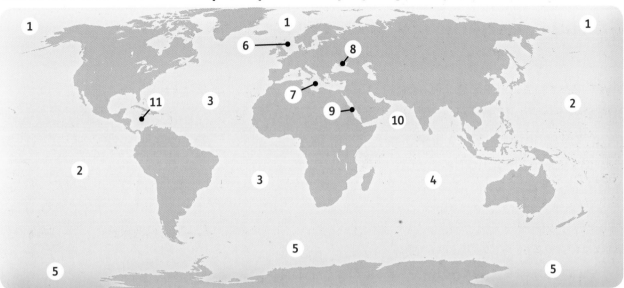

1 L'océan Arctique *Arctic Ocean*	**5** L'océan Austral *Southern Ocean*	**9** La mer Rouge *Red Sea*
2 L'océan Pacifique *Pacific Ocean*	**6** La mer du Nord *North Sea*	**10** La mer d'Arabie *Arabian Sea*
3 L'océan Atlantique *Atlantic Ocean*	**7** La mer Méditerranée *Mediterranean Sea*	**11** La mer des Caraïbes *Caribbean Sea*
4 L'océan Indien *Indian Ocean*	**8** La mer Noire *Black Sea*	

La haute mer
Open ocean

le hareng
herring

le poisson volant
flying fish

Les mers profondes
Deep seas

le loup de mer
wolf fish

le calmar vampire
vampire squid

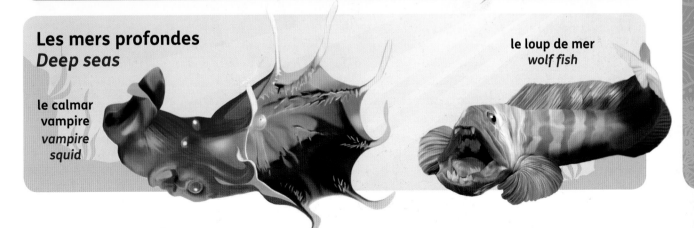

87

Au bord de la mer
On the seashore

Les animaux du bord de mer vivent sur le sable et les rochers submergés par la mer à marée montante. Des oiseaux marins volent le long de la côte à la recherche de nourriture.

Seashore creatures live on sand and rocks that are covered by sea when the tide comes in. Seabirds fly along the shore looking for food.

❶ l'huîtrier pie
oystercatcher

❷ le cormorant
cormorant

❸ le crabe
crab

❹ la crevette
shrimp

❺ l'étoile de mer
starfish

❻ l'oursin
sea urchin

❼ les moules
mussels

❽ l'anémone de mer
sea anemone

❾ le bernard l'hermite
hermit crab

❿ les patelles
limpets

⓫ les balanes
barnacles

⓬ le macareux
puffin

⓭ la mouette
seagull

La vie dans l'océan

Dans l'océan • *In the ocean*

Des milliers d'espèces de poissons vivent dans les océans. Les poissons de petite taille nagent habituellement en groupes, appelés bancs, alors que les plus grands poissons chassent seuls.

Thousands of species of fish live in the oceans. Smaller fish usually swim in groups, called shoals, while larger fish hunt alone.

1 la sardine • *sardine*	**4** le poisson pilote • *pilot fish*	**7** le flétan • *halibut*
2 le maquereau • *mackerel*	**5** le flet • *flounder*	**8** la sole • *sole*
3 la plie, le carrelet • *plaice*	**6** le barracuda • *barracuda*	**9** la roussette • *dogfish*

Life in the ocean

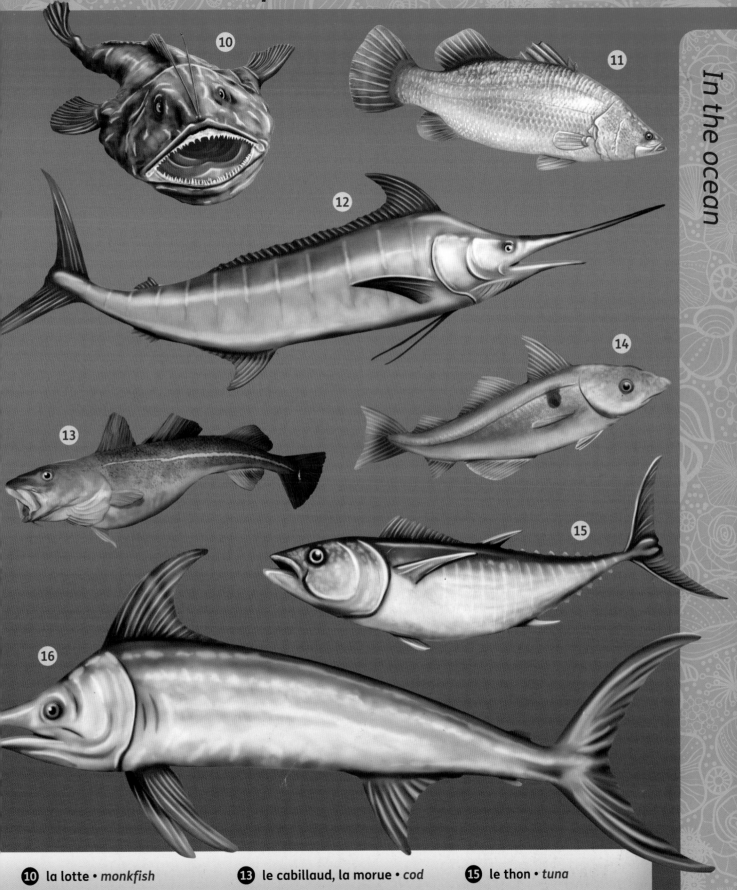

10 la lotte • *monkfish*

11 le bar, le loup • *sea bass*

12 le marlin • *marlin*

13 le cabillaud, la morue • *cod*

14 l'aiglefin • *haddock*

15 le thon • *tuna*

16 l'espadon • *swordfish*

D'autres animaux des océans
More ocean life

Quelques très grands animaux vivent dans l'océan. Les baleines, les dauphins, les marsouins, les lamantins et les dugongs sont tous des mammifères. Les requins et les raies sont des poissons.

The ocean is home to some very large creatures. Whales, dolphins, porpoises, manatees and dugongs are all mammals. Sharks and rays are fish.

le dauphin • *dolphin*
Les dauphins utilisent des sons, comme les clics et les sifflets, afin de communiquer les uns avec les autres.
Dolphins use sounds, such as clicks and whistles, to communicate with each other.

le lamantin
manatee

le requin-marteau
hammerhead shark

le grand requin blanc
great white shark
Le grand requin blanc peut vivre jusqu'à l'âge de 70 ans.
A great white shark can live to be as old as 70.

la raie manta
manta ray

le dugong • *dugong*
Les dugongs broutent la végétation des fonds sous-marins peu profonds.
Dugongs graze on seagrasses on shallow sea beds.

le marsouin • *porpoise*
Les baleines, les dauphins et les marsouins respirent par leur évent.
Whales, dolphins and porpoises breathe though a blow hole.

Les baleines • *Whales*

la baleine à bosse
humpback whale

l'orque • *orca*
On prête à l'orque le surnom
de baleine tueuse.
*The orca is also known as
the killer whale.*

la baleine bleue • *blue whale*
La baleine bleue est le plus grand animal de la Terre.
The blue whale is the largest animal on Earth.

le cachalot • *sperm whale*

Les baleines à fanons, les mysticètes • *Baleen whales*

Certaines baleines ont leur bouche garnie de poils appelés des fanons. Les fanons permettent de retenir de minuscules créatures marines, telles que le plancton et le krill.
Some whales have flexible bristles called baleen inside their mouths. The baleen plates trap tiny sea creatures, such as plankton and krill.

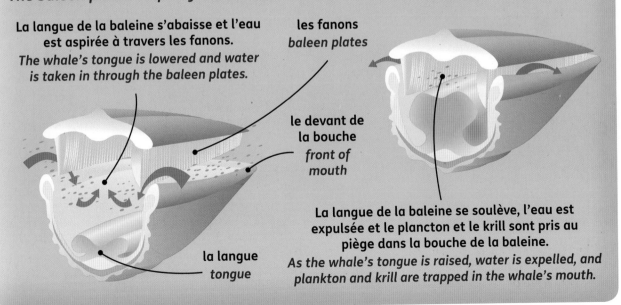

La langue de la baleine s'abaisse et l'eau est aspirée à travers les fanons.
The whale's tongue is lowered and water is taken in through the baleen plates.

les fanons
baleen plates

le devant de la bouche
front of mouth

La langue de la baleine se soulève, l'eau est expulsée et le plancton et le krill sont pris au piège dans la bouche de la baleine.
As the whale's tongue is raised, water is expelled, and plankton and krill are trapped in the whale's mouth.

la langue
tongue

Les récifs de corail • *Coral reefs*

Les récifs de corail sont des constructions animales vivantes ! Les polypes coralliens sécrètent leur propre squelette. Quand le corail meurt, son squelette reste et l'accumulation de ces squelettes forme progressivement un récif.

Coral reefs are made from living creatures! Coral polyps grow a hard outer case. When the coral dies, the casing remains and gradually builds up to form a reef.

le poisson-ange
angelfish

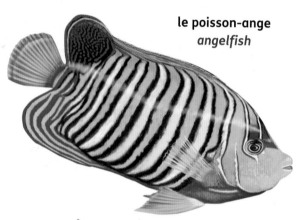

la porcelaine • *cowry*
La porcelaine est une espèce de gastéropode marin.
The cowry is a species of sea snail.

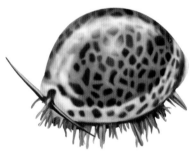

l'hippocampe
seahorse
L'hippocampe mâle porte ses petits dans une poche.
The male seahorse carries its young in a pouch.

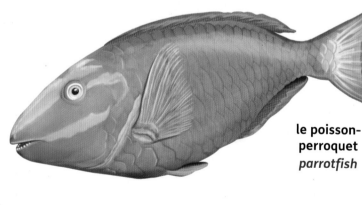

le poisson-perroquet
parrotfish

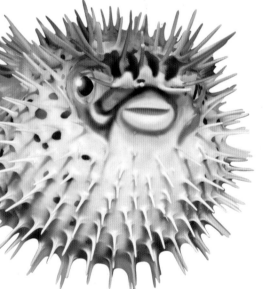

le poisson-ballon,
le poisson-globe • *puffer fish*
Lorsqu'il est menacé, le poisson-ballon se gonfle en avalant de l'eau.
When it is threatened, the puffer fish expands by swallowing water.

le bénitier géant
giant clam

Life in the ocean

**la tortue verte,
la tortue franche**
green turtle

le poisson-clown
clown fish

le baliste
triggerfish

le poisson-papillon
butterfly fish

le poisson-demoiselle
damselfish

**le pennatule,
la plume de mer**
sea pen
Le pennatule se nourrit
de plancton.
*Sea pens feed on
plankton.*

l'ophiure
brittle star

**le barbier du récif,
l'anthias rouge**
sea goldie

la rascasse volante
lion fish

Les créatures des profondeurs • *Creatures of the deep*

Il fait presque complètement noir au fond de l'océan, cependant certaines créatures des profondeurs peuvent créer leur propre lumière. D'autres ont des yeux très grands qui les aident à voir.

It is almost completely dark on the ocean bed, but some deep-sea creatures can create their own light. Others have very large eyes to help them see.

1. **la hache d'argent** • *hatchetfish*

2. **l'anguille des sources** • *vent fish*

3. **le poisson-lanterne** • *lantern fish*

4. **le poisson-pêcheur** • *angler fish*

5. **les vers tubicoles géants** • *tube worms*

6. **les éponges des grandes profondeurs** • *deep-sea sponges*

Life in the ocean

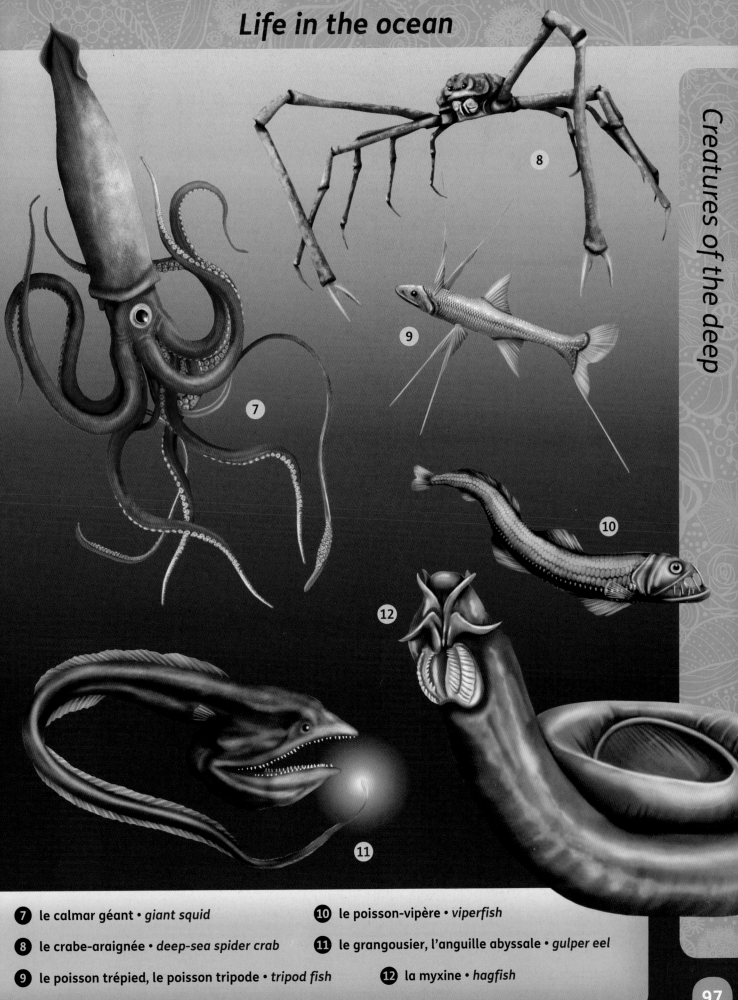

7 le calmar géant • *giant squid*

8 le crabe-araignée • *deep-sea spider crab*

9 le poisson trépied, le poisson tripode • *tripod fish*

10 le poisson-vipère • *viperfish*

11 le grangousier, l'anguille abyssale • *gulper eel*

12 la myxine • *hagfish*

97

Sur la calotte glaciaire arctique, les ours polaires partent à la chasse...

On the Arctic ice-cap, polar bears go hunting...

LES ANIMAUX DES RÉGIONS POLAIRES
ANIMALS OF THE POLAR REGIONS

Les animaux des régions polaires

Les habitats polaires • *Polar habitats*

Les régions arctiques et antarctiques sont constituées principalement de glace et de roche. L'Arctique est une mer gelée encerclée d'une terre à moitié gelée appelée toundra.

The Arctic and Antarctic regions are mostly ice and rock. At the edge of the ice are freezing seas and semi-frozen land, known as tundra.

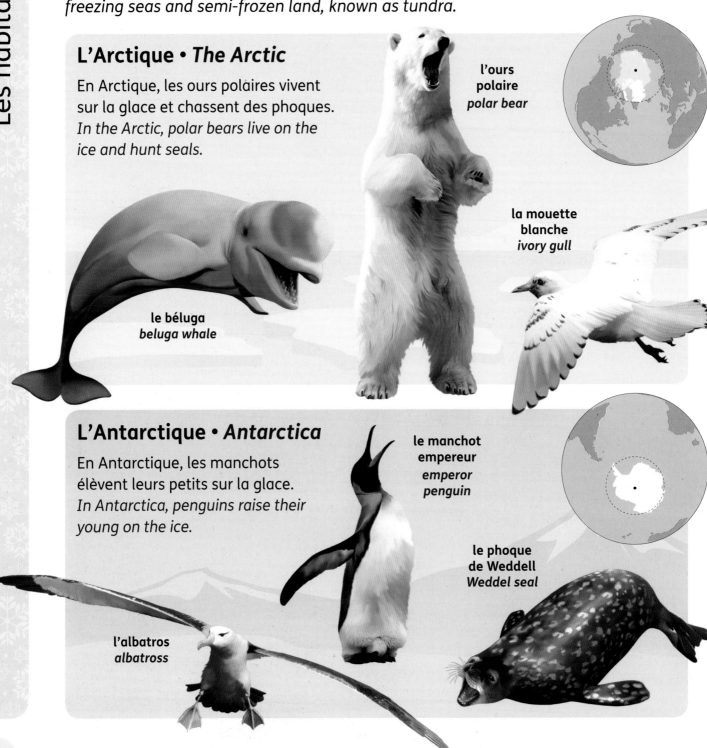

L'Arctique • *The Arctic*

En Arctique, les ours polaires vivent sur la glace et chassent des phoques.
In the Arctic, polar bears live on the ice and hunt seals.

l'ours polaire
polar bear

la mouette blanche
ivory gull

le béluga
beluga whale

L'Antarctique • *Antarctica*

En Antarctique, les manchots élèvent leurs petits sur la glace.
In Antarctica, penguins raise their young on the ice.

le manchot empereur
emperor penguin

le phoque de Weddell
Weddel seal

l'albatros
albatross

100

Animals of the polar regions

Carte des régions polaires • *Map of the polar regions*

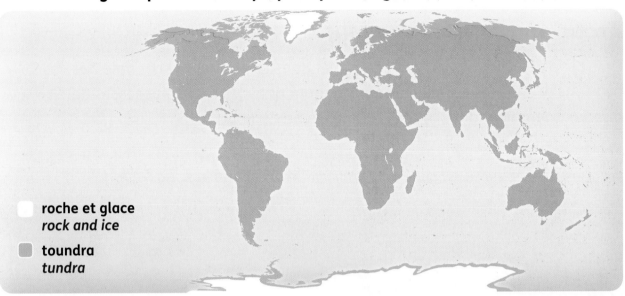

☐ **roche et glace**
rock and ice

▨ **toundra**
tundra

Les régions de la toundra • *Tundra regions*

Les régions de la toundra sont recouvertes de neige une grande partie de l'année.
The tundra regions are covered in snow for the most of the year.

le loup arctique
Arctic wolf

la bernache du Canada
Canada goose

l'hermine
ermine

Les animaux des régions polaires

La faune de l'Arctique et de l'Antarctique
Arctic and Antarctic wildlife

On trouve des phoques dans l'Arctique et dans l'Antarctique. Les baleines, les poissons et d'autres animaux marins nagent dans les mers glacées, et des oiseaux tournoient dans le ciel à la recherche de nourriture.

Seals are found in the Arctic and in Antarctica. Whales, fish and other sea creatures swim in the icy seas and birds circle overhead looking for food.

le labbe parasite
Arctic skua

le morse
walrus

le phoque annelé, le phoque marbré • *ringed seal*
Les phoques possèdent une épaisse couche
de lard qui les protège du froid.
*Seals are protected from the cold by a thick
layer of fat known as blubber.*

le gorfou sauteur
rockhopper penguin

la raie arctique
Arctic skate

102

Animals of the polar regions

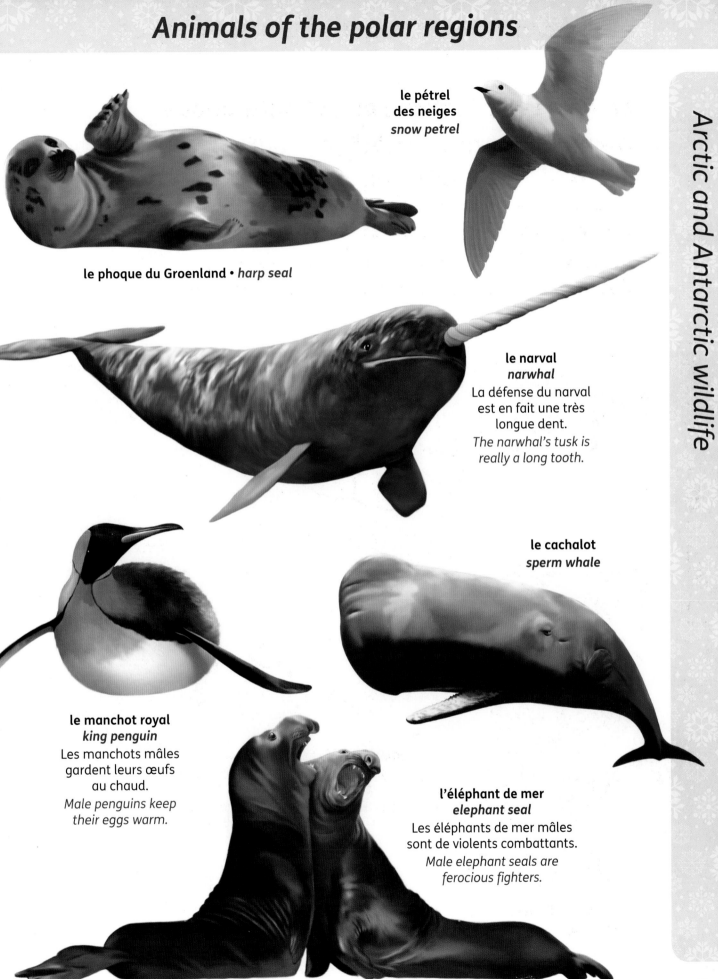

le pétrel des neiges
snow petrel

le phoque du Groenland • *harp seal*

le narval
narwhal
La défense du narval est en fait une très longue dent.
The narwhal's tusk is really a long tooth.

le cachalot
sperm whale

le manchot royal
king penguin
Les manchots mâles gardent leurs œufs au chaud.
Male penguins keep their eggs warm.

l'éléphant de mer
elephant seal
Les éléphants de mer mâles sont de violents combattants.
Male elephant seals are ferocious fighters.

103

La vie dans la toundra • *Life in the tundra*

Les régions de la toundra ont de très courts étés. Quand la neige fond, certains animaux perdent leur manteau d'hiver, d'autres sortent de leur terrier où ils s'étaient abrités.

Tundra regions have very short summers. When the snow thaws, some animals shed their winter coats and some emerge from burrows where they have sheltered.

le lièvre arctique
Arctic hare

le caribou
caribou
Les caribous sont aussi connus sous le nom de rennes.
Caribou are also known as reindeer.

l'oie des neiges
snow goose

l'eider à duvet
eider duck
Les eiders à duvet ont des plumes très douces, appelées « duvet », qu'ils utilisent pour tapisser leurs nids.
Eider ducks have very soft feathers called down that they use to line their nests.

le lemming arctique
Arctic lemming

Animals of the polar regions

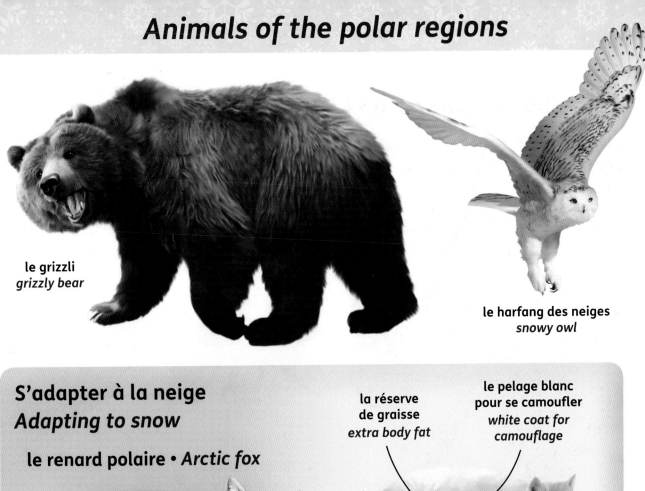

le grizzli
grizzly bear

le harfang des neiges
snowy owl

S'adapter à la neige
Adapting to snow

le renard polaire • *Arctic fox*

la réserve
de graisse
extra body fat

le pelage blanc
pour se camoufler
*white coat for
camouflage*

en été
summer

en hiver
winter

de la fourrure
sous les pattes
fur on base of paws

le manteau long et
hirsute du dessus
long, shaggy overcoat

le bœuf musqué • *musk ox*

en été
summer

la toison laineuse
du dessous
fleecy undercoat

de lourds sabots pour creuser la neige
heavy hooves to break through snow

en hiver
winter

105

Les animaux très répandus

On retrouve certains animaux dans une grande variété d'habitats à travers le monde. Parmi ces petites créatures très répandues on trouve de nombreuses espèces d'insectes et de petits invertébrés.

Some animals are found in a wide range of habitats across the world. These widespread creatures include many species of insects and minibeasts.

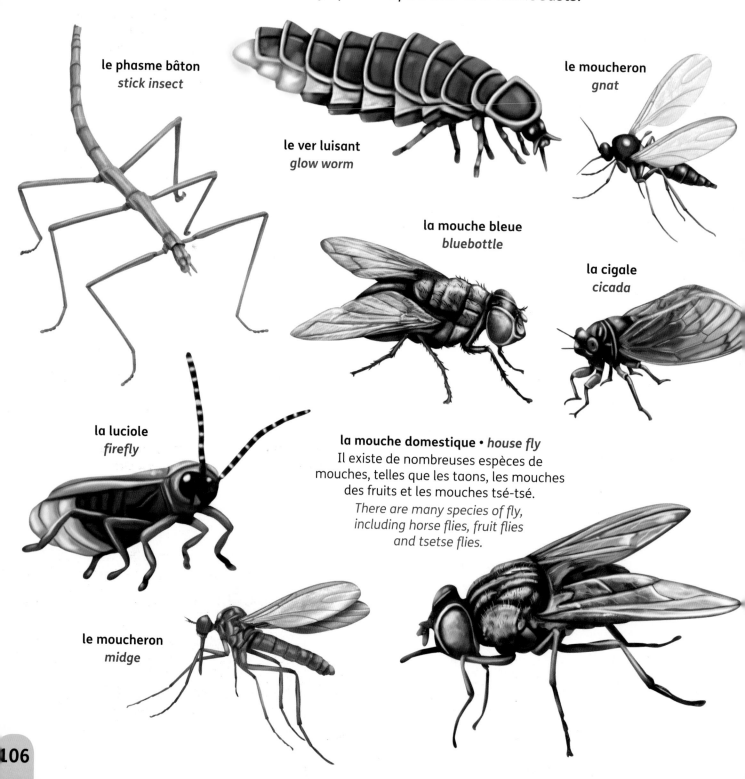

le phasme bâton
stick insect

le ver luisant
glow worm

le moucheron
gnat

la mouche bleue
bluebottle

la cigale
cicada

la luciole
firefly

la mouche domestique • *house fly*
Il existe de nombreuses espèces de mouches, telles que les taons, les mouches des fruits et les mouches tsé-tsé.
There are many species of fly, including horse flies, fruit flies and tsetse flies.

le moucheron
midge

Widespread creatures

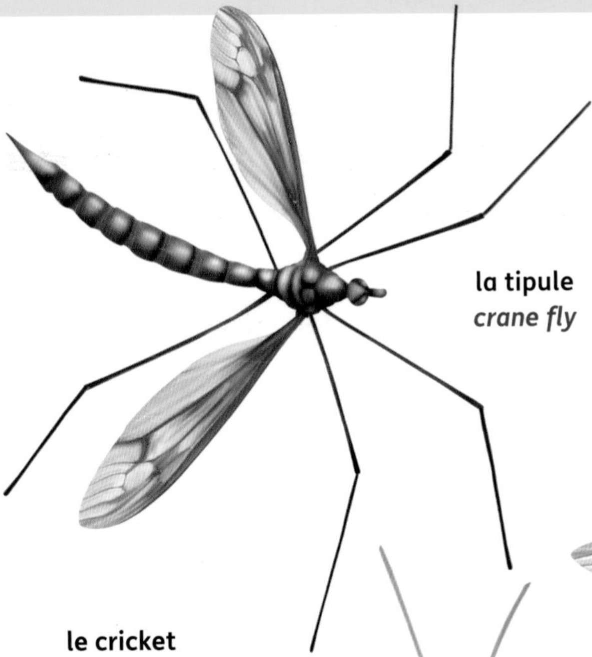

la tipule
crane fly

la piéride du chou, le papillon
blanc du chou
cabbage white butterfly

le cricket
cricket

la guêpe
wasp

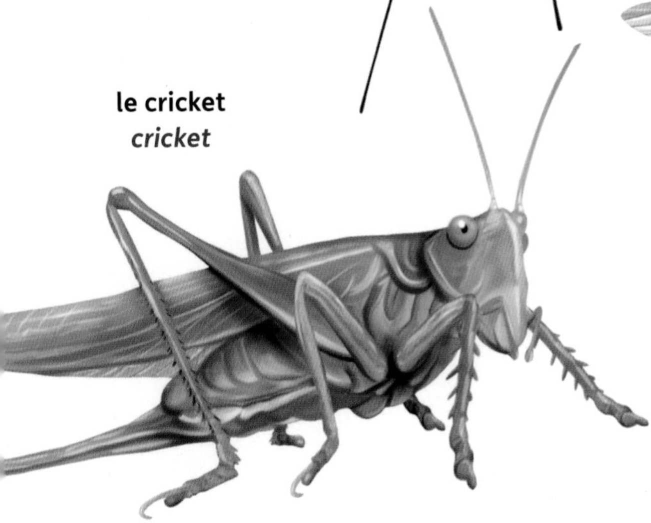

le frelon
hornet

la coccinelle
ladybird

le perce-oreille
earwig

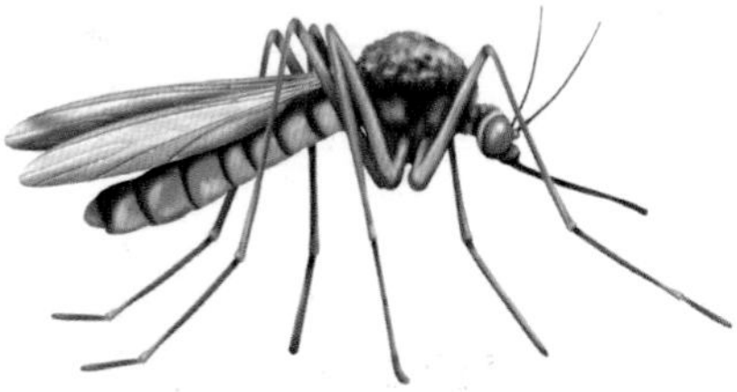

le moustique
mosquito

le cafard
cockroach

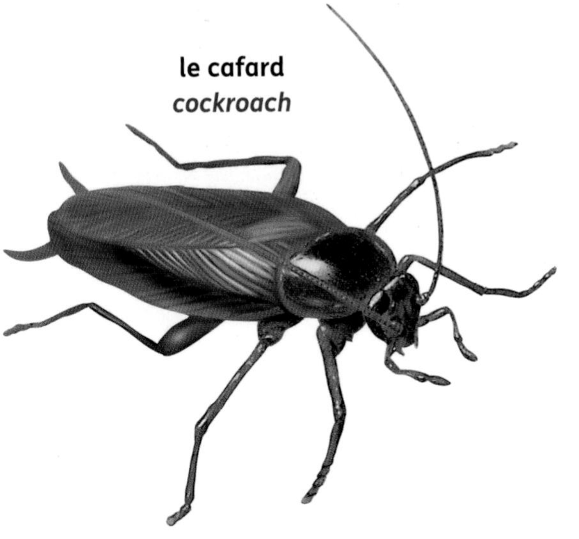

le bousier
dung beetle

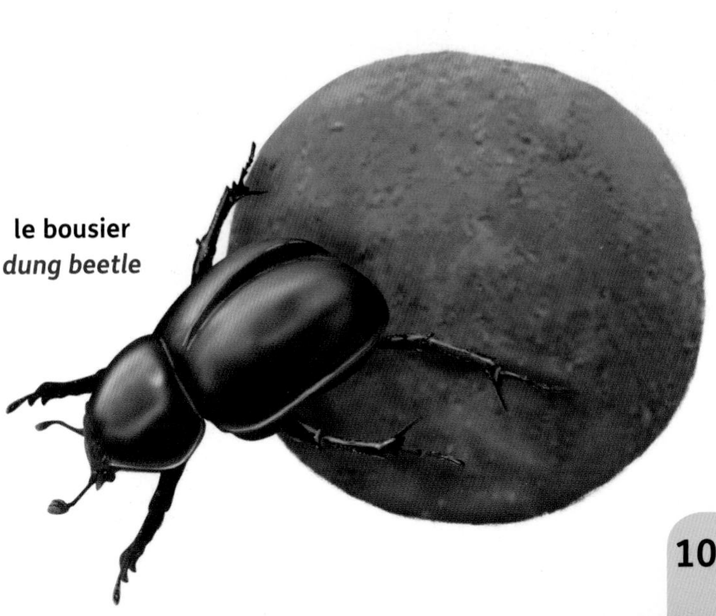

Les oiseaux très répandus

Certaines espèces d'oiseaux se trouvent dans de nombreuses régions du monde. En voici quelques exemples.

Some types of bird are found in many parts of the world. Here are some common examples.

le choucas
jackdaw
Les choucas appartiennent à la famille des corvidés.
Jackdaws belong to the crow family.

le pinson des arbres • *chaffinch*
Le pinson des arbres appartient à la famille des fringillidés. Cette famille comprend le bouvreuil et le chardonneret.
The chaffinch belongs to the finch family. Other finches include the bullfinch and the goldfinch.

le coucou
cuckoo

la grive
thrush

le paon • *peacock*
Les paons sont gardés comme animaux de compagnie dans de nombreuses régions du monde. Ils vivent à l'état sauvage en Afrique et en Asie.
Peacocks are kept as pets in many parts of the world. They live in the wild in Africa and Asia.

Widespread birds

l'alouette des champs
skylark

le moineau
sparrow

l'étourneau
starling

le merle
blackbird

le cygne • *swan*
Les cygnes australiens sont noirs.
Australian swans are black.

le troglodyte mignon
wren

le pigeon • *pigeon*
Les pigeons vivent en grand
nombre dans les villes.
*Pigeons are found in large
numbers in cities.*

la tourterelle turque
collared dove

la pie
magpie

109

Comment s'appellent les bébés des animaux ?

What do you call a baby animal?

ANIMAL	JEUNE
ANIMAL	*YOUNG*
l'aigle	l'aiglon
eagle	*eaglet*
l'anguille	la civelle
eel	*elver*
l'antilope	le faon
antelope	*calf*
l'araignée	bébé
spider	*spiderling*
la baleine	le baleineau
whale	*calf*
la belette	la jeune belette
weasel	*kit*
le blaireau	le blaireautin
badger	*cub*
le brochet	le brocheton / le poignard
pike	*pickerel*
le buffle / le bison	le veau
buffalo	*calf*

le caribou	le faon
caribou	*fawn*
le castor	le bébé
beaver	*kit*
le chameau	le chamelon
camel	*calf*
le cheval	le poulain / la pouliche
horse	*foal / colt (male) / filly (female)*
le chien	le chiot
dog	*puppy / pup / whelp*
la chouette	la jeune chouette
owl	*owlet*
le couguar	le chaton
cougar	*kitten*
le coyote	le chiot
coyote	*puppy*
le crapaud	le têtard
toad	*tadpole*
le cygne	le jeune cygne
swan	*cygnet*

Animal words

l'éléphant	**l'éléphanteau**	**l'ours**	**l'ourson**
elephant	*calf*	*bear*	*cub*
le furet	**le fureton**	**le phoque**	**le blanchon / le chiot / le veau**
ferret	*kit*	*seal*	*calf / pup*
la girafe	**le girafeau / le girafon**	**le pigeon**	**le pigeonneau**
giraffe	*calf*	*pigeon*	*squab / squeaker*
la grenouille	**le têtard**	**le poisson**	**l'alevin**
frog	*tadpole*	*fish*	*fry*
le kangourou	**le joey / le bébé**	**le rhinocéros**	**le bébé**
kangaroo	*joey*	*rhinoceros*	*calf*
le lièvre	**le levraut**	**le saumon**	**le tacon / le saumonneau**
hare	*leveret*	*salmon*	*parr / smolt*
le lion	**le lionceau**	**le tigre**	**le tigreau**
lion	*cub*	*tiger*	*cub*
le loup	**le louveteau**	**wallaby**	**le joey / le bébé**
wolf	*cub / pup / whelp*	*wallaby*	*joey*
le lynx	**le bébé / le chaton**	**le zèbre**	**le zébreau**
bobcat	*kitten*	*zebra*	*foal*
le morse	**le veau**		
walrus	*cub*		
l'oie	**l'oison**		
goose	*gosling*		

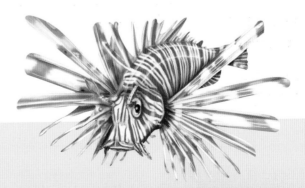

Comment appelle-t-on un groupe... ?

What do you call a group of...?

d'abeilles	**un essaim**
bees	*a swarm*
de baleines	**un groupe**
whales	*a pod*
de dauphins	**un groupe**
dolphins	*a school*
de fourmis	**une colonie**
ants	*a colony*
de lions	**une harde / un groupe / une meute**
lions	*a pride*
de loups	**une meute**
wolves	*a pack*
d'oies	**un troupeau**
geese	*a gaggle / a flock*
d'oiseaux	**une volée**
birds	*a flock*
de poissons	**un banc**
fish	*a shoal / a school*
de singes	**un groupe**
monkeys	*a troop*

Animal words

Quel bruits font les animaux ?

What noise does an animal make?

Les abeilles bourdonnent
ou vrombissent.
Bees buzz.

Les ânes braient.
Donkeys bray.

Les canards cancanent ou nasillent.
Ducks quack.

Les chevaux hennissent.
Horses neigh and whinny.

Les chiens aboient, jappent, hurlent,
grondent ou clabaudent.
Dogs bark and growl.

Les chouettes ululent, huent
ou chuintent.
Owls hoot.

Les éléphants barèrent ou barrient.
Elephants trumpet.

Les grenouilles coassent.
Frogs croak.

Les lions rugissent.
Lions roar.

Les loups hurlent.
Wolves howl.

Les oiseaux chantent, pépient,
gazouillent, babillent, ramagent
ou sifflent.
Birds sing, tweet, warble and chirp.

Les perroquets asent ou craquent.
Parrots screech.

Les poules caquettent, gloussent
ou crétellent.
Hens cluck.

Les serpents sifflent.
Snakes hiss.

Les singes crient, hurlent ou paillent.
Monkeys chatter.

Les souris chicotent ou couinent.
Mice squeak.

Les vaches beuglent, meuglent
ou mugissent.
Cows moo.

Le quiz des animaux

Que sais-tu des animaux ? Remplis le quiz des animaux en les cherchant dans les pages de ce livre. Les réponses sont à la fin du livre.

How much do you know about animals? Try this animal detective quiz by tracking down the creatures in the pages of this book. The answers are at the back of the book.

Les chasseurs d'animaux
Animal hunters

1. Quel animal injecte ses victimes de salive mortelle ?

Which creature injects its victims with deadly saliva?

2. Quel animal suce le sang de plus grands animaux ?

Which creature sucks blood from larger animals?

3. Quel animal étourdit sa proie par un choc électrique ?

Which creature stuns its prey with an electric shock?

Attention !
Watch out!

4. Quel animal met en garde ses attaquants en produisant une odeur très forte ?

Which animal warns off attackers by producing a very strong smell?

5. Quel animal met en garde ses attaquants en avalant de l'eau pour paraître plus grand ?

Which animal warns off attackers by swallowing water to make itself look larger?

6. Quel animal met en garde ses attaquants en affichant des couleurs d'avertissement pour montrer qu'il est toxique ?

Which animal warns off attackers by displaying warning colours to show it is poisonous?

Particularités
Special features

7. Quel animal possède des plaques osseuses couvrant son corps ?

Which creature has bony plates covering its body?

8. Quel animal possède d'énormes oreilles qui lui permettent de perdre rapidemment de la chaleur ?

Which creature has enormous ears that can lose heat fast?

Animal detective quiz

9. Quel animal possède une longue langue qui lui permet de sucer le nectar ?

Which creature has a long tongue for sucking nectar?

Un comportement inhabituel
Unusual behaviour

10. Quel animal peut courir sur la surface de l'eau ?

Which animal can run on the surface of water?

11. Quel animal communique à l'aide de clics et de sifflets ?

Which animal communicates by using clicks and whistles?

12. Quel animal dort environ 20 heures par jour ?

Which animal sleeps for around 20 hours a day?

Les habitats des animaux
Animal homes

13. Quel animal vit dans une hutte ?

Which creature lives in a lodge?

14. Quel animal construit son habitat avec de la terre et de la salive ?

Which creature builds a home from earth and saliva?

15. Quel animal vit dans les intestins d'autres animaux ?

Which creature lives inside the guts of other animals?

Les parties des animaux
Animal parts

16. Quel animal possède une filière ?

Which animal has a spinneret?

17. Quel animal possède un sac vocal ?

Which animal has a dewlap?

18. Quel animal possède un siphon ?

Which animal has a siphon?

Qui suis-je ?
What am I?

19. Je suis un mammifère qui pond des œufs.

I am a mammal that lays eggs.

20. Je suis un poisson qui peut respirer sur la terre.

I am a fish that can breathe on land.

Index français • *French index*

Index français • *French index*

Index français • *French index*

Index français • *French index*

Index anglais • *English index*

Index anglais • English index

crane   76
crayfish   70
crimson rosella   50
crocodile   20, 70
crusher claw   24
cuttlefish   86
damselfish   95
damselfly   68
deciduous forest   41-43
deep-sea creatures   87, 96-97
deep-sea spider crab   97
deep-sea sponges   96
deer   40, 42
desert tortoise   81
Desert wildlife   78-83
dewlap   22
diamondback terrapin   77
dingo   64
dipper   72
dog   16
dogfish   91
dolphin   92
domesticated creatures   53
dormouse   44
dorsal fin   24
dragonfly   72
dromedary camel   82
drone   27
duck   19, 104
dugong   92
eagle   18, 31, 52
ear   16
eardrum   22
earthworm   44
eel   71, 97
egg   18, 27, 61, 71
elder duck   104
electric eel   71
elephant   33, 59
emerald tree boa   31
emergent layer   30
emperor moth   62

emperor penguin   100
emu   65
ermine   101
evergreen forest   41
eye   16, 25
eye stalk   24
eyelash viper   34
falcon   52
fallow deer   40
feather   18
fennec fox   80
ferret   63
fin   24
finger   17
fish and other sea creatures   24-25, 84-97
flamingo   74
flank   16
flipper   20
Florida panther   77
flounder   90
flying dragon lizard   30
flying fish   87
flying gecko   35
foot   17
foreleg   16
Forest and woodland wildlife   38-47
forest floor   30
forewing   27
forked end tongue   21
fox   43, 80, 105
frog   22, 23, 30, 35, 72, 74
frog spawn   23
funnel web spider   32
galah   65
garden snail   40
gazelle   56
gecko   35
gerbil   82
giant anteater   30
giant clam   94
giant panda   53

giant rainforest praying mantis   34
giant squid   97
giant tube worm   96
gibbon   31
gill cover   24
gills   23, 25
giraffe   59
giraffe weevil   35
goanna   57
goat   50
golden eagle   52
goldfish   75
goliath beetle   31
goliath spider   33
goose   19, 101
gorilla   33, 51
grasshopper   63
Grassland wildlife   54-65
great grey owl   47
great hornbill   30
greater water boatman   73
green iguana   36
green turtle   95
grey squirrel   43
grizzly bear   105
grouse   62
guinea fowl   62
haddock   91
hagfish   97
halibut   90
hammerhead shark   92
hare   63, 104
harpy eagle   31
hatchetfish   96
hawk owl   41
head   25, 26
heart   17
hedgehog   44
Hercules beetle   32
Hermann's tortoise   21
heron   19, 72
herring   87

Index anglais • English index

Index anglais • English index

Les réponses du quiz

Les chasseurs d'animaux
Animal hunters

Attention !
Watch out!

Particularités
Special features

Un comportement inhabituel
Unusual behaviour

Quiz answers

11. le dauphin   **(p. 92)**
dolphin

12. le paresseux à trois doigts   **(p. 37)**
three-toed sloth

Les habitats des animaux
Animal homes

13. le castor   **(p. 71)**
beaver

14. la termite   **(p. 61)**
termite

15. le ténia   **(p. 10)**
tapeworm

Les parties des animaux
Animal parts

16. l'araignée   **(p. 26)**
spider

17. la grenouille   **(p. 22)**
frog

18. le poulpe   **(p. 25)**
octopus

Qui suis-je ?
What am I?

19. le platypus   **(p. 71)**
platypus

20. le dipneuste   **(p. 76)**
lungfish